UNDERSTANDING FRANK LLOYD WRIGHT'S ARCHITECTURE

DONALD HOFFMANN

DOVER PUBLICATIONS, INC.
New York

ACKNOWLEDGMENTS

For their various instances of help and patience in affording me access to Wright's buildings, providing illustrations, furnishing information and, most of all, encouraging a project at first so nebulous and hence so long in gestation, I wish to thank Donald P. Hallmark, Lynda Waggoner, Virginia Ernst Kazor, Jeffrey M. Chusid, August Oliver Brown, Howard W. Ellington, James Dennis, Mildred Rosenbaum, Maya Moran, Minerva Montooth, Richard Carney, Suzette Lucas, Bruce Brooks Pfeiffer, Oscar Muñoz, Indira Berndtson, Sidney K. Robinson, Curtis Besinger, Jack Quinan, James O'Gorman, Sarah Bradford Landau, Paul E. Sprague, John Eifler, Robert Kostka, Charles Biederman, Nicolette Bromberg, Carolyn De Witt Koenig, Dorothy H. Shields, Steve Wyatt, Shonnie Finnegan, my brothers George Hoffmann, John Hoffmann and Fred Hoffmann, and my friends Harry Haskell, Edgar Tafel, Ellen Goheen, Elpidio Rocha, Pamela Kingsbury and Robin Jefferies Younger.

D. H.

Copyright

Bibliographical Note

Understanding Frank Lloyd Wright's Architecture is a new work, first published by Dover Publications, Inc., in 1995.

Library of Congress Cataloging-in-Publication Data

Hoffmann, Donald.
Understanding Frank Lloyd Wright's architecture / Donald Hoffmann.
p. cm.
Includes index.
ISBN 0-486-28364-X (pbk.)
1. Wright, Frank Lloyd, 1867–1959—Criticism and interpretation. I. Title.
NA737.W7H63 1995
720'.92—dc20 94-42767
CIP

Book design by Carol Belanger Grafton

Manufactured in the United States of America
Dover Publications, Inc., 31 East 2nd Street, Mineola, N.Y. 11501

CONTENTS

LIST OF ILLUSTRATIONS

INTRODUCTION

The literature about Frank Lloyd Wright, now so vast, remains largely unsatisfactory. Wright fought for principles, not mere details or idiosyncrasies, and yet very few commentaries even ask what those principles might be. What inspired his work? How did his architecture mature? What are the dynamics of its characteristic expression? Why will the formative principles always be valid?

Observations about Wright commonly fail to reach any understanding of his art. Such formulations as "flowing space" and "ribbon windows" and "overhanging eaves" persist not only as clichés but as insipid, inaccurate, worthless little phrases. Plainly enough, space is not liquid and does not flow; instead, it is moved through, bodily or with the eyes, imagination and memory. The noble spaces in Wright's architecture consist of highly structured vistas—oblique perspectives that change with each slight shift or turn and lure the mind toward what is just out of sight. A "ribbon window" ought to describe only a narrow, unpunctuated, smooth surface of glass. But the windows in Wright's buildings are both vital and articulate; they open outward and break free from the uniform plane. The words "overhanging eaves," apart from their obvious redundancy, cannot begin to suggest the sheer generative energy of projection in his roofs and cornices.

To begin afresh with Wright is to reject the accumulated burden of received opinion, all the academic theories that pretend to explain his architecture from presumed methods and sources, whether from the Froebel kindergarten toys his mother so proudly claimed credit for giving him (although he was already nine years old), or the Arts and Crafts movement, the Vienna Secession, manipulations of grid systems or tartan plaids into ground plans, playful exercises in pure abstraction (clearly in advance of Cubism, but somehow dependent on European modernism for validation), archetypal memories or sophomoric Freudian symbols, arcane literary allusions or even dreamlike condensations of motifs cunningly harvested from the whole history of architecture (as if an art on this order could have been constructed upon a foundation of footnotes).

To respond to each of those theories would only compound the pedantry beyond which Wright never fails to soar. Goethe remarked the absurdity of scholars who avoid the living concept to concern themselves merely with what others have said about it. Otto von Simson writes in *The Gothic Cathedral* that those who overrate and oversimplify such assumed influences, seeking in art history a consistent and predictable course, take the sure road to misunderstanding all that is significant, original and authentic. Nothing more directly kills the productive capacity in art, said Schelling, than a concentration on memory. Or, as Pope nicely put it:

> Where beams of warm imagination play,
> The memory's soft figures melt away.

Much that has been published about Wright's life and work remains trivial, repetitive or irrelevant. Critical inquiry too quickly gives way to historical narrative, history lapses into biography, and, to pander to what Plato called the ignorant multitude, biography descends into rumor and gossip. The art itself goes unexamined.

Buildings stand still, but Wright could invest them with the force of movement and with an aesthetic integrity that evoked organic growth. The visual dynamics of his work will be understood only after the informing principles have been grasped. Wright always meant to be an exemplar, not a teacher. Averse to school and rule, he said it was not his task to assess or interpret his own work; moreover, he was intensely competitive and thus far from eager to expose his innermost procedure. His writing grew discursive and too often beside the point. Hence his words need to be sifted and weighed with care, sifted again and always tested against the evidence of the eye. Then they will help to identify the principles that gave his architecture not only its extraordinary vigor of structure and form, expression and meaning, but its surprising continuity.

THE ROMANCE OF THE HORIZONTAL

Surely it was from Louis H. Sullivan, the architect he most respected other than himself, that Frank Lloyd Wright gained for his art its purpose and its probity. Paradoxically, he needed nothing at all from Sullivan's architecture. Echoes of Sullivan's work in fact diminished Wright's early buildings, just as Wright's work later produced a backwash in Sullivan's. This complex relation between master and pupil Wright came to describe with great poignancy in the memoir he titled *Genius and the Mobocracy*. What had Sullivan, then, that proved of such consequence for Wright? Three things: an undiluted concept of the architect as an artist, a high intellectual regard for nature and a fervent desire to create for America an architecture of its own. Thus directed in his life's work, Wright could revere the master as a man of great principle and at the same time submit the master's architecture to the most unsparing of critiques. No one saw Sullivan's weaknesses so clearly as Wright. "The buildings he has left with us for a brief time," Wright said, "are the least of him."[1]

Despite the abiding affection he professed for nature, Sullivan found the natural materials of building inert and inorganic. They had to be "organized and vitalized," he wrote, "in order that a real building may exist." Sullivan had little empathy for the inherent virtues of materials, their distinctive strengths and different voices. Wright saw that he treated brick, stone, wood, iron and plaster as if all were the same, and all destined to be impressed with the fluent and often florid ornamentation best left to baked clay, or terra-cotta. To regard architecture as a triumph of spirit over matter, Wright said, was to assume a false and fatal division of the house against itself: "A greater triumph will be man's when he triumphs through the nature of matter over the superstition that separates him from its spirit." An architect, said Wright, should train himself to see that every material possesses a poetry of its own, hence becomes its own ornamentation and even suggests the appropriate proportions for a building. Sullivan considered architecture a spiritualization of matter, but Wright saw it as the materialization of spirit. As early as 1900, the architect Robert C. Spencer, Jr., wrote that Wright's feeling for the sources of beauty in materials was extraordinary. And in 1924, at the very end of his life, Sullivan

[1]Wright, *An Autobiography* (New York, 1943), p. 269; also see *Genius and the Mobocracy* (New York, 1949), passim.

graciously conceded that Wright possessed "an apprehension of the material, so delicate as to border on the mystic, and yet remain coördinate with those facts we call real life."[2]

Nor did Sullivan give much attention to the other fundamental aspects of architecture: the structural system and the effects of space. The imaginative and eccentric R. M. Schindler, who for a few years worked for Wright, once described Sullivan as an architect "who has not yet understood completely the third dimension." Wright himself wondered about Sullivan's preoccupation with plasticity in ornament. "Why a principle working in the part," he asked, "if not living in the whole?" Moreover, the obvious naturalism of the make-believe plant forms in Sullivan's ornament betrayed a preliminary stage in the imitation of nature. Sullivan thus left himself vulnerable, Wright said, to an "insidious sentimentality." An imagination that could stay within the realm of geometric invention was bound to be more architectonic. Wright also discerned that Sullivan lacked an awareness of the implications of the machine in architecture and failed to see in plate glass, steel and reinforced concrete the latent poetics of the modern. The ancient tradition of the masonry arch still seemed to Sullivan the most eligible and emotional of structural principles.[3]

Undiminished by all those shortcomings, Sullivan's force of character gave Wright every encouragement to hold nature in the highest esteem. At his distant country retreat in Mississippi, for which Wright had designed the simple cottage and stables, Sullivan lived almost engulfed by plant life, and in *Kindergarten Chats*, his most important book, he continually preached a nature doctrine. Nature provided a metaphor "infinite of interpretation." Nature signified fertility, chastity, strength, generosity, beauty, mobility, subtlety and serenity. Nature's powers and deeds possessed "exquisite logic." And nature remained the "one unfailing source." To have removed man from nature, Sullivan said, was the great crime of education:

> The great minds may go to the great cities but they are not (generally speaking) born and bred in the great cities. In the formation of a great mind, a simple mind, a master mind, solitude is prerequisite; for such a mind is nurtured in contemplation, and strengthened in it. In the quiet, in the silence, alone with itself and Nature. . . . All great thought, all great ideas, all great impulses, are born in the open air, close to Nature, and are nursed, all unknown, all unsuspected, upon Nature's bosom.[4]

In most of what Wright read he found the master's thoughts confirmed, indeed prefigured. The outdoor spirit—particularly if opposed to the squalor of the modern industrial city—was very much in the air. For one, Ruskin wrote that "the Power of human mind had its growth in the Wilderness," and he recommended that an architect

---

[2]Louis H. Sullivan, *Kindergarten Chats* [1918] (Dover reprint, New York, 1979), p. 140; Baker Brownell and Frank Lloyd Wright, *Architecture and Modern Life* (New York, 1937), p. 61, and Wright, "In the Cause of Architecture: The Meaning of Materials—Stone," the *Architectural Record* 63 (April 1928), p. 355; Sullivan, "Reflections on the Tokyo Disaster," the *Architectural Record* 55 (February 1924), p. 116.

[3]Esther McCoy, *Vienna to Los Angeles: Two Journeys* (Santa Monica, Calif., 1979), p. 130, and Wright, *An Autobiography*, pp. 146, 103.

[4]Sullivan, *Kindergarten Chats*, pp. 89, 108, 201, 133, 159, 196, 112.

"live as little in cities as a painter." Nietzsche warned that in the mire of the city "great thoughts are boiled alive and cooked till they are small." Thoreau gave thanks for the "indescribable innocence and beneficence of Nature." Whitman pronounced democracy the younger brother of nature:

> Now I see the secret of the making of the best persons,
> It is to grow in the open air and to eat and sleep with the earth.[5]

The more that Wright read, the more he saw his adolescence in a new light; now he could look back to his long summers on the family farmlands of southern Wisconsin not simply as a time of hard work and moral growth but as an intimate introduction to the aesthetics of nature. Nature—whether in microcosm or in landscape—achieved the absolute repose of "destiny fulfilled." Creatures, trees, flowers and weeds, Wright said, flourished as glorious exemplars of organized form. If the organic approach to art was as old as Aristotle, it could nonetheless inspire every generation with fresh energies. Wright heard Sullivan talk of nature's eloquence of organization, and he already knew the words of Viollet-le-Duc:

> Nature, in all her works, has style, because, however varied her productions may be, they are always submitted to laws and invariable principles. The lilies of the field, the leaves of the trees, the insects, have style, because they grow, develop, and exist according to essentially logical laws. We can spare nothing from a flower, because, in its organization, every part has its function and is formed to carry out that function in the most beautiful manner. Style resides in the true and well-understood expression of a principle, and not in an immutable form; therefore, as nothing exists in nature without a principle, everything in nature must have style.

Wright could see that nature had nothing to do with fashion but always attained style, or what he described as the poetic expression of intrinsic character—"the result of an organic working out of a project in character and in one state of feeling." Measured against such a standard, American architecture appeared incoherent. "The average desire," Wright said as early as 1894, "seems to be to build something which will rear on its hind legs and paw the air in order that you may seem more important than your neighbor." Most buildings of the Victorian era conspicuously insulted the land upon which they so awkwardly stood [Fig. 1]. Victorian architecture, Wright wrote later, was a failed architecture:

> What was the matter with the house? Well, just for a beginning, it lied about everything. It had no sense of unity at all nor any such sense of space as

[5]John Ruskin, *The Seven Lamps of Architecture* (London, 1849), pp. 141, 99; F. W. Nietzsche, *Thus Spoke Zarathustra* [1883–92], tr. Walter Kaufmann (New York, 1966), p. 176; Henry David Thoreau, *Walden* [1854], ed. J. W. Krutch (New York, 1962), p. 207; Walt Whitman, "Song of the Open Road" [1855], in *The Portable Walt Whitman*, ed. Mark Van Doren (New York, 1973), p. 159.

1. Victorian house on the prairie.

> should belong to a free people. It was stuck up in any fashion . . . . To take any one of those so-called homes away would have improved the landscape and cleared the atmosphere.[6]

So far as the terms of art, the typical Victorian house looked hopeless; and yet its eruption of bays and turrets, the nooks and rooms that broke off rambunctiously from other rooms, at least defied the tradition of foursquare, genteel and boxy buildings. Wright

---

[6]Wright, "A Philosophy of Fine Art" [1900], in *Collected Writings*, vol. 1, ed. B. B. Pfeiffer (New York, 1992, p. 43; E.-E. Viollet-le-Duc, *Discourses on Architecture*, tr. Henry Van Brunt (Boston, 1875), p. 179; Wright, A *Testament* (New York, 1957), p. 225; *Ausgeführte Bauten und Entwürfe von Frank Lloyd Wright* [1910] (Dover reprint, New York, as *Drawings and Plans of Frank Lloyd Wright: The Early Period [1893–1909]*, 1983); in *Collected Writings*, vol. 1, pp. 108, 110; Wright, "The Architect and the Machine" [1894], in *Collected Writings*, vol. 1, p. 22; Wright, "Two Lectures on Architecture" [1931], in *Collected Writings*, vol. 2 (New York, 1992), p. 85.

For the impact of Viollet on Wright, see my essay "Frank Lloyd Wright and Viollet-le-Duc," *Journal of the Society of Architectural Historians* 28 (October 1969), pp. 173–183.

faced the task of finding a potent source of aesthetic discipline for a better species of freedom. If the products of nature presented exemplars of form, what lessons might reside in the landscape itself? Wright discovered the catalyst to new principles of architectural expression only after he chose to invoke the lost prairies of the Middle West. This was his finest moment with nature.

The prairies had been a strangely open land, devoid of human settlement and altogether lacking in trees or any other features by which to measure distance, scale or direction. Impressed by such vast expanses of grasses and wildflowers, early travelers often recalled the grandest parks in England. Some worried, however, about a soil that seemed unable to produce trees; but the prairie earth soon proved exceedingly rich. Its tangles of grassy roots could shatter cast-iron implements. Settlers in Illinois used as many as eight oxen for a first plowing, and found that without sowing again they could harvest a second crop of wheat at forty bushels to the acre. Reports reached far abroad; no one wrote more profoundly of the prairies than a man who had never seen them, the philosopher Schopenhauer:

> Let us imagine ourselves transported to a very lonely place, with unbroken horizon, under a cloudless sky. . . . Such surroundings are, as it were, a call to seriousness and contemplation, apart from all will and its cravings; but this is just what imparts to such a scene of desolate stillness a touch of the sublime. For, because it affords no object, either favorable or unfavorable, for the will, which is constantly in need of striving and attaining, there only remains the state of pure contemplation, and whoever is incapable of this, is ignominiously abandoned to the vacancy of unoccupied will, and the misery of ennui. So far it is a test of our intellectual worth, of which, generally speaking, the degree of our power of enduring solitude, or our love of it, is a good criterion.[7]

The fate of the wild prairie landscape was unhappily forced by its very fertility; after the invention of the steel plow, what was once touched with the sublime gave way to the banal economics of agriculture. William Cullen Bryant traveled in Illinois in 1841, and wrote of a landscape "spreading away on every side until it met the horizon." Five years later, when he returned, he found "the road for long distances now passed between fences, the broad prairie, inclosed, was turned into immense fields of maize, oats and wheat." He also noted that settlers often fell prey to mysterious fevers from which they contracted powerful feelings of guilt:

> It is a common remark in this country, that the first cultivation of the earth renders any neighborhood more or less unhealthy. "Nature," said a western

[7]Arthur Schopenhauer, *The World as Will and Representation*, vol. 1 [1819, 1844], in *Philosophies of Art and Beauty*, ed. A Hofstadter and R. Kuhns (Chicago, 1964), p. 463.

Such is the power of an idea unencumbered by experience. In the *Critique of Aesthetic Judgment*, Kant writes that to be sufficient to oneself, without shunning society, is something "approaching the sublime." Nietzsche writes of his own energy "to choose absolute solitude," and Montaigne declares that only in solitude can man know true freedom.

2. Prairie landscape, 1902.

> man to me, some years since, "resents the violence done her, and punishes those who first break the surface of the earth with the plough."

Just as Wright began to find his own voice, at the turn of the century, Hamlin Garland published his popular reminiscence titled *Boy Life on the Prairie*. Garland wrote that by 1884 the landscape of northern Iowa, a state once more occupied by prairies than any other, had become a different world. No open prairies could be found and the wildflowers were gone. Wright was born in 1867 and for the most part raised at the edge of the prairies. He witnessed the very years when the virgin landscape disappeared.[8]

---

[8]William Cullen Bryant, *Letters of a Traveller* (New York, 1850), pp. 55, 262–63, 267; Hamlin Garland, *Boy Life on the Prairie* (Boston, 1899), p. 416. Garland's book was so popular it continued through eight editions.

From that loss, came the birth of a prairie spirit: an afterglow of poetic nostalgia for such scenes of quiet beauty and broad significance as the image of freedom. Before he began to shape his buildings in full consciousness of the prairie spirit, Wright was a skilled and accomplished architect but hardly a great one. In his project to redeem the lost landscape through an architecture conceived as its abstract equivalent, or analogue, he discovered the principles that would inform his art for the rest of his life.

Wright's progress was slow and unsteady and often far from evident. His romance with the landscape began long before he took hold of the principles that became so formative. At first, he liked to say, he had only been feeling his way, knowing that some better relation between buildings and the land had to be possible. Emerson observed that in every landscape the point of astonishment occurred where earth met sky; but only on the prairie was that intersection so grand and uninterrupted [2]. In 1833, a New England merchant journeyed to northern Illinois and noted in his diary what he saw:

> The country about Chicago, for the distance of twelve miles from the lake, is mostly a low prairie covered with grass and beautiful flowers. Southwest from the town there is not one tree to be seen; the horizon rests upon the prairie.

Boy Life on the Prairie sounded the same theme. The prairies had been "wide, sunny, windy country," Garland wrote, where "the sky was so big and the horizon line so low and so far away."[9]

Louis Sullivan spoke of "a dream born of the incomparable Lake and the strong, silent, lovely prairies." But it was a dream he never made clear, just as he never made the horizontal the leading motif of his architecture. To regard Sullivan as the founder of a "Prairie School" would be nothing less than grotesque, Wright wrote in 1915 to Wilhelm Miller, who in that year published a tract on the prairie spirit offered free to anyone in Illinois who promised to undertake some permanent ornamental planting. Miller lamented the loss of the wild prairies. "How can men restore flowers and poetic suggestion to a land nearly ninety percent of which is tilled?" he asked. His answers came mainly from the landscape architect Jens Jensen, whom Wright knew. In public parks and on private estates Jensen invoked the prairie spirit by planning broad meadows bordered by native trees, many of which responded to the prairie horizon in the stratified disposition of their limbs. "For years the message of our great prairies had appealed to me," Jensen once recalled. "Every leisure moment found me tramping through unspoiled bits of these vast areas. I wanted to understand their force, their enchantment that called on and on." The prairies had impressed Jensen as early as 1885, wrote Miller, but it was 1901 before he engaged in his first large prairie design.[10]

Wright said he found Jensen to be a lovable soul and one possessed of a true grasp of

---

[9]Colbee C. Benton, in *Prairie State*, ed. Paul M. Angle (Chicago, 1968), p. 114; Garland, *Boy Life on the Prairie*, p. 9.

[10]Sullivan, *Kindergarten Chats*, p. 111; Wright, *Letters to Architects*, ed. B. B. Pfeiffer (Fresno, Calif., 1984), p. 50; Wilhelm Miller, *The Prairie Spirit in Landscape Gardening* (Urbana, Ill., 1915), p. 3; Jens Jensen, *Siftings* [1939] (Chicago, 1956), p. 75.

the "peculiar charm of our prairie landscape." But he also thought that Jensen imitated nature much too literally, and told him so:

> . . . I think you would be interested to see how a minority report, such as I might bring in with my experience in the study of structural Form as interpretation of nature, would compare with yours . . . .
>
> You are a realistic landscapist. I am an abstractionist seeking the pattern behind the realism—the interior structure instead of the comparatively superficial exterior effects you delight in. In other words I am a builder. You are an effectivist using nature's objects to make your effects.

Even at the turn of the century Wright had deplored naturalistic art and its "gasping poverty of imitative realism." Architecture was a more useful art and at the same time more abstract. It could easily outdistance what he later would call the "subgeometric." If the prairie horizon rarely appeared as a straight line, it nonetheless gave birth to the lengthened horizontal—an abstraction with the full potency of a generative architectural idea.[11]

Any house, Wright said in 1894, should appear to be part of its site "and not a foreign element set up boxwise on edge to the utter humiliation of every natural thing in sight." His early work failed to emphasize the horizontal consistently, but only because he had not yet formed a clear idea of how the lost prairies might inspire a new aesthetic. But by 1900 Robert C. Spencer, Jr., could write of the "evident love for the horizontal dimension and the horizontal line" in Wright's buildings, and note that "long lines are obtained whenever possible." Early the next year, with the publication of his project for "A Home in a Prairie Town" in the *Ladies' Home Journal*, Wright acknowledged his source [3, 4]:

> The exterior recognizes the influence of the prairie, is firmly and broadly associated with the site, and makes a feature of its quiet level. The low terraces and the broad eaves are designed to accentuate that quiet level and complete the harmonious relationship.

Wright told his associates in 1903 he was "thoroughly saturated with the spirit of the prairie," and in the March 1908 issue of the *Architectural Record* published his classic statement:

> We of the Middle West are living on the prairie. The prairie has a beauty of its own and we should recognize and accentuate this natural beauty, its quiet level. Hence, gently sloping roofs, low proportions, quiet sky lines, sup-

[11]Wright, *Letters to Architects*, p. 22; "Chicago Culture" [1918], in *Collected Writings*, vol. 1, p. 157; *Letters to Architects*, p. 104; "The Art and Craft of the Machine" [1901], in *Collected Writings*, vol. 1, p. 61; *An Autobiography*, p. 157.

"A picture or poem," Ruskin writes, "is often little more than a feeble utterance of man's admiration of something out of himself; but architecture approaches more to a creation of his own, born of his necessities, and expressive of his nature"; see *The Stones of Venice*, vol. 2 (London, 1853), p. 180.

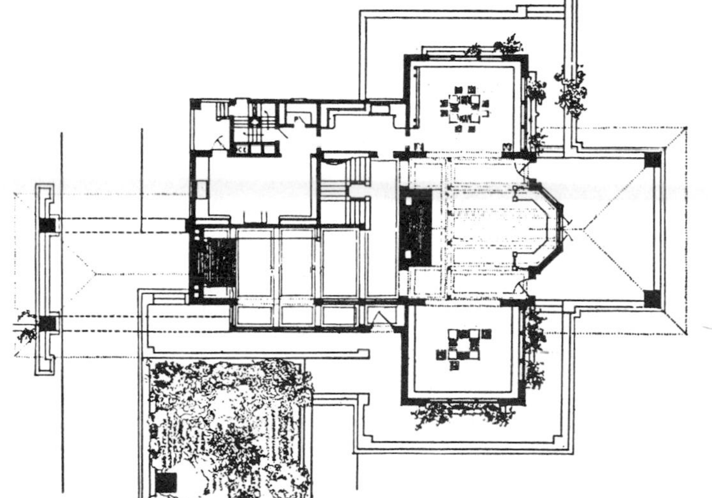

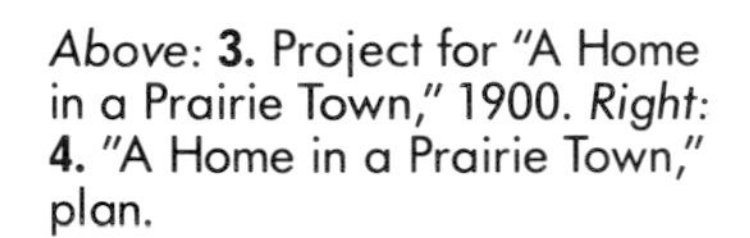

Above: **3.** Project for "A Home in a Prairie Town," 1900. *Right:* **4.** "A Home in a Prairie Town," plan.

pressed heavy-set chimneys and sheltering overhangs, low terraces and out-reaching walls sequestering private gardens.

In 1910, for the portfolio of his work printed by Ernst Wasmuth in Berlin, Wright wrote that his buildings and projects respected "an ancient tradition, the only one here worthy of respect—the prairie."[12]

[12]Wright, "The Architect and the Machine," p. 21; Robert C. Spencer, Jr., "The Work of Frank Lloyd Wright," *Architectural Review* 7 (June 1900), pp. 63–64, 67; Wright, "A Home in a Prairie Town," *Ladies' Home Journal* 18 (February 1901), p. 17; "Letters, 1903–1906, by Charles E. White, Jr., from the Studio of Frank Lloyd Wright," ed. N. K. Morris Smith, *Journal of Architectural Education* 25 (1971), p. 104; Wright, "In the Cause of Architecture," the *Architectural Record* 23 (March 1908), p. 157; *Ausgeführte Bauten und Entwürfe*, in *Collected Writings*, vol. 1, p. 113.

The wild prairies were lost, but the lay of the land stayed the same; and if the prairie horizon forever seemed remote, intangible as a rainbow, the long horizontal could be realized instantly as the most elementary mark from pencil and T-square. The basic tools of architectural design, Wright said, suited him perfectly. Strictly geometric design could take him beyond his early imitations of Sullivan's freehand style, its simulations of plant life and suggestions of sentimentality, and keep him free as well from the nostalgia implicit in any celebration of the lost landscape. His romance of the horizontal would always be ruled by what he called the "more severe rhythms of point, line and plane." Hence the lengthened horizontal was never a mere imitation of the prairie. It was an idea, a vital abstraction.[13]

A building impelled by the horizontal took its place on the land with great flair. "I had an idea (it still seems to be my own) that the planes parallel to the earth in buildings identify themselves with the ground, do most to make the buildings belong to the ground," Wright said. Parallel horizontals—all horizontals being either parallel or coincident—reinforced one another and, to Wright's eye, gave the building its grip on the earth. Parallel horizontals introduced new effects of spaciousness, and lowered proportions to a scale in harmony with human dignity and intimacy. Straight lines and sharp planes spoke, too, of machine technology and of the new speed of travel and communication. In 1900, long before the architect Le Corbusier proclaimed the dawn of modernity, Wright wrote of a beauty "as organic and clean a revelation of natural conditions as a dynamo—an engine, or a battleship."[14]

Wright had found in the horizontal a new force for a new architecture in the New World. It brought to his vision of landscape and architecture a rare, invincible optimism:

> . . . we may yet see the Machine Age as the age of a true democracy, wherein human life is based squarely on and in the beauty and fruitfulness of the ground: life lived in the full enjoyment of the earthline of human life—the line of freedom for man, whereby man's horizon may be immeasurably extended by the machine . . . .

The open landscape was nature's eloquent way of making freedom visible. If buildings, too, could speak directly of freedom, the one great ideal shared by the broad and heterogeneous American people, they could achieve what Louis Sullivan had only dreamed of.[15]

---

[13]Wright, *An Autobiography*, pp. 103, 104; *Genius and the Mobocracy*, p. 55.

[14]Wright, "Organic Architecture" [1936], in *Frank Lloyd Wright on Architecture*, ed. Frederick Gutheim (New York, 1941), p. 179; Wright, "A Philosophy of Fine Art," p. 40.

Viollet-le-Duc cites as an exemplar of true style the expression of "controlled power" in a locomotive, and J.-K. Huysmans, in his 1884 novel *A Rebours*, asserts that a locomotive is more beautiful than the female form.

[15]Wright, "Two Lectures on Architecture," p. 91.

ROOF, CANTILEVER AND RIFT

Frank Lloyd Wright often said his buildings were like plants that grew from within and came up from the ground into the light. But his work had developed from the outside in and from the top down. Such was a paradox that has gone almost unnoticed: His mature way of thinking about architecture lay opposite the way he took to architectural maturity.

Wright first of all wished to bring architecture into harmony with the land. Hence he had every reason to begin his reforms in the outward look of a building. Its ground plan, academic opinion to the contrary, did not at first play a crucial role; buildings of vastly different appearance, after all, could be constructed from the very same plan. Robert C. Spencer, Jr., saw in 1900 that although Wright consistently tried to reduce the number of rooms on the main floor of a house, this was "not, generally speaking, an original or peculiar idea." Visitors from abroad had been quick to remark that the principal rooms in many American houses opened to one another with a surprising informality and freedom. And when he described his own work in 1908, Wright was refreshingly candid:

> The exteriors of these structures will receive less ready recognition perhaps than the interiors and because they are the result of a radically different conception as to what should constitute a building. We have formed a habit of mind concerning architecture to which the expression of most of these exteriors must be a shock, at first more or less disagreeable . . ..

The ground plans, he said, were "merely the actual projection of a carefully considered whole." Many years later he wrote of the "originating idea of modern architecture from the outside in" and fondly recalled the "new shapes of shelter" he had published in Germany in 1910 and 1911:

> Quiet mass-outlines extended upon the ground levels in becoming human proportions throughout . . . the early straight-line, flat-plane dwellings built by myself—happily and with great hope—on the midwest prairie I loved . . .. The plan grew more beneficial to human life.

The originating idea proceeded from the outside in, he said, and served to "get the house down in the horizontal to appropriate proportion with the prairie."[1]

---

[1]Spencer, "The Work of Frank Lloyd Wright," p. 67; Wright, "In the Cause of Architecture," pp. 163, 161; *A Testament*, pp. 131, 86, 202; "Two Lectures on Architecture," p. 86.

What happened at the roof and eaves gave the first sure sign that Wright was out to make an architecture all his own. In 1624, Henry Wotton wisely said of the roof that "though it be the last of this *art* in execution, yet it is always in *intention* the first, for who would build but for *shelter?*" Life in the Middle West demanded shelter; the weather, as Wright said, changed from bitter cold to simmering heat, from long months of drought to sudden downpours, thunderstorms and even tornadoes:

> Alternate extremes of heat and cold, of sun and storm, have also to be considered. The frost goes four feet into the ground in winter; the sun beats fiercely on the roof with almost tropical heat in the summer: an umbrageous architecture is almost a necessity, both to shade the building from the sun and protect the walls from freezing and thawing moisture, the most rapidly destructive to buildings of all natural causes.

Spencer in 1900 took pains to explain why Wright almost invariably exaggerated the eaves. They excluded the sun from the upper rooms during the hotter hours of a summer day, he wrote, and provided shade for five or six months of the year. Their soffits, or undersurfaces, reflected indoors a diffused light as agreeable as it was surprising. And as the roof surfaces quieted the whole, the eaves brought a satisfying sense of shelter from sun and storm.[2]

But the eaves were only an effect of the radically assertive roof. Wright's attention to the roof and his affection for the horizontal—both inspired by his feeling for the prairies—had happily coincided. To salute the landscape he projected the roof decisively past the walls and thus exalted the necessary into the poetic:

> The climate, being what it was, a matter of violent extremes of heat and cold, damp and dry, dark and bright, I gave broad protecting roof-shelter to the whole . . . . At this time, a house to me was obviously primarily an interior space under fine *shelter*. I liked the sense of shelter in the "look of the building." I achieved it, I believe.[3]

Wright lowered the roof, lengthened it and brought it closer to the ground [5]. Nothing so distinguished his Prairie years as the expressive power he gave to the roof [6]. And in the best projects from the very end of his career—such as those of 1957 for the Arizona State Capitol and of 1959 for a Fair Pavilion at the Marin County Civic Center—the life of the roof still proved characteristic. In his 1908 manifesto, significantly, he wrote first of the roof and then of the foundation and stylobate, the arrangement of the wall up to sill and frieze, the window groups, the plan, ornament, function, relation to client and, last of all, the interior and its furnishings. In the same paper he classified his buildings by roof type, a Japanese custom. (Long before 1905, when Wright first visited Japan, Edward

[2]Henry Wotton, *The Elements of Architecture* (London, 1624), p. 78; Wright, *Ausgeführte Bauten und Entwürfe*, p. 112; Spencer, "The Work of Frank Lloyd Wright," p. 68.

[3]Wright, *Modern Architecture* (Princeton, N.J., 1931), p. 70.

Above: **5.** A new sense of the roof. Project for Elizabeth Stone summer cottage, Glencoe, Illinois, about 1906. *Below:* **6.** The power of the roof. Taliesin, the architect's home and studio near Spring Green, Wisconsin, 1911–59.

S. Morse had written that "it is mainly to the roof that the Japanese house owes its picturesque appearance." The extended eaves, Morse observed, were meant to protect the paper shoji screens from rain.) And many of the most engaging drawings Wright published in his Wasmuth portfolio of 1910 were bird's-eye renderings, which so beautifully illustrated the shape and spirit of his broad sheltering roofs [7]. Much later, Wright pondered the history of architecture, and said the general aspect of man's earliest dwellings was most affected by the shape of the roof:

> Later the sense of roof as shelter overcame the sense of walls, and great roofs were to be seen with walls standing back in under them . . .. His roof was not only his shelter, it was his dignity, as well as his sense of home . . . the roof-shelter became the most important factor in the making of the house. It became the ultimate feature of his building. This remains true to this late day.[4]

The outline of the roof could reveal much of the character and sometimes even the identity of a building [8]. Thus when he quoted the derisive words of Thoreau—"A sentimental reformer in architecture, he began at the cornice, not at the foundation"—Wright curiously compounded the irony. For it was precisely at the cornice that he began to show his hand, and he had confessed as much at Princeton University in 1930, when he spoke about the cornice almost obsessively. The cornice had become an ornamental vestige, he declared, and a useless emblem of ancient gratitude for the overhanging foliage that once protected mankind from sun and rain. But the cornice could be transformed:

> Instinctive gratitude is of course fainter now. But whenever the Cornice, true to that primeval instinct, was *real shelter* or even the sense of it, and dropped roof-water free of the building walls—well, the Cornice was not a Cornice then but was an overhanging *roof*. Let the overhanging roof live as human shelter. It will never disappear from Architecture. The sense of Architecture as human shelter is a very fine sense—common sense, in fact.[5]

By tradition, the cornice emphasized the top of the wall, just as the roof formed the lid on a building, and, in Palladio's phrase, served as a kind of ligament to the whole. Together, the cornice and roof closed the building, making it a boxlike vessel for a limited and specific volume. Wright chose to set asunder what tradition so firmly joined; he changed the conclusion of the building into a beginning, a vital zone of lateral thrust into the landscape.

---

[4]Edward S. Morse, *Japanese Homes and Their Surroundings* [1886] (Dover reprint, New York, 1961), pp. 77, 242; Brownell and Wright, *Architecture and Modern Life*, pp. 25–26.

[5]Wright, in the *Architectural Forum* 68 (January 1938), facing p. 1, quoting from Thoreau, *Walden*, p. 139; Wright, *Modern Architecture*, p. 53.

Thoreau was alluding to the sculptor and essayist Horatio Greenough, whose thoughts on architectural ornamentation he dismissed in his journal entry for January 11, 1852, as little better than "the common dilettantism." In *An Autobiography*, p. 142, Wright speaks of "getting back to the purpose for which the cornice was originally designed."

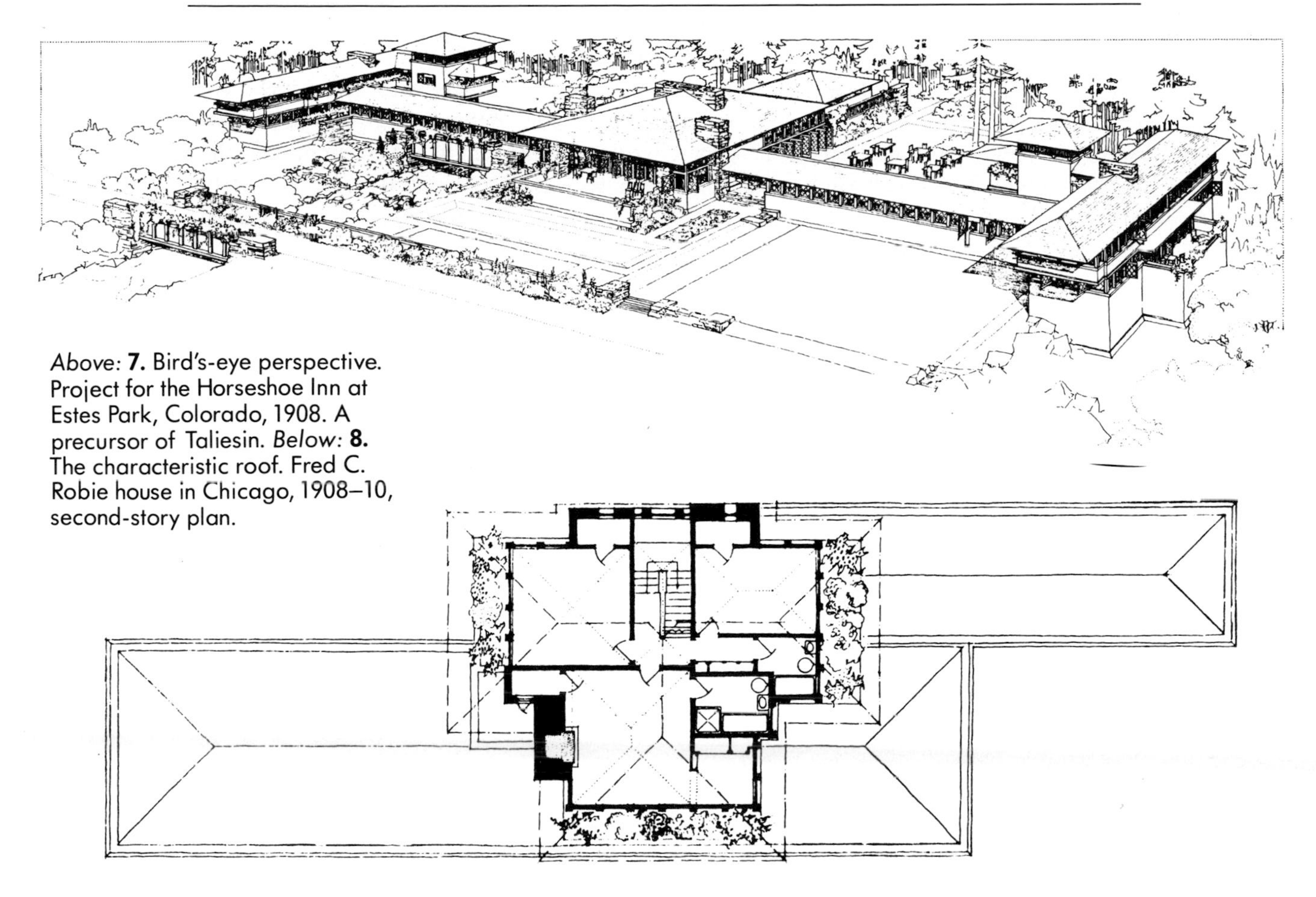

Above: **7.** Bird's-eye perspective. Project for the Horseshoe Inn at Estes Park, Colorado, 1908. A precursor of Taliesin. *Below:* **8.** The characteristic roof. Fred C. Robie house in Chicago, 1908–10, second-story plan.

To achieve this radical reversal he relied on the cantilever, a significant projection of structure beyond any base or point of direct support. As he recognized the latent expressive power of the cantilever, Wright grasped his first formative principle. Nothing but the cantilever could so daringly assert the horizontal or so grandly culminate a series of planes parallel to the earth. The force of a cantilever might well be compared with that of a running figure; the more a figure leans forward, as Leonardo observed, the swifter it appears, and a moving figure looks faster the farther its center of gravity takes leave from its center of support. Hence all the promise in the house Wright built for himself in 1889 came from the strength of the overscaled gable that already advanced past the wall [9]. (The extent to which the house resembled certain suburban houses designed earlier by Bruce Price was of no significance whatever.) A few years later, Wright made the roofs of a boathouse on Lake Mendota in Madison, Wisconsin, reach five feet past the walls [10]. And in his 1905 project for another boathouse in Madison he cantilevered the roof twice that far [11].[6]

[6]For detailed accounts of the boathouses, see John O. Holzhueter, "The Lakes Mendota and Monona Boathouses" and "The Yahara River Boathouse," in *Frank Lloyd Wright and Madison*, ed. Paul E. Sprague (Madison, Wis., 1990), pp. 29–44.

Wright reinforced the horizontal of the cantilevered roof by reorganizing the wall into long courses, or what the German architect Erich Mendelsohn described as a "layered arrangement of the masses." If the stratification of the wall sometimes looked awkward, even amusing, it was because Wright divided the wall not at the second floor but at the second-story sill, which made the building look high-waisted. The horizontal divisions nevertheless represented the first step toward a liberation and diversification of the wall into what he would call light-screens and wall-screens. Charles E. White, Jr., an early assistant, in 1904 accurately reported Wright's procedure:

> His grammar, which he may be said to have invented, is such as he used in the Winslow house, consisting of a base, a straight piece of wall up to the second story window sills, a frieze from this front to the roof, and a cornice with a wide overhang . . ..

Opposite: **9.** The advancing roof. House for the architect, Oak Park, Illinois, 1889 (studio addition, at left, 1898). *Above:* **10.** The cantilevered roof. Lake Mendota Boathouse, Madison, Wisconsin, 1893. *Below:* **11.** The cantilevered roof. Yahara River Boathouse project, Madison, Wisconsin, 1905.

Note how everything is in simple square planes in keeping with the horizontal and perpendicular lines of the house, while the angle in the plan repeats the shape of the roof. Thus everything throughout the house is in the same feeling. When he designs glass, iron-work, furniture, fixtures, etc., he first analyzes the type of his building, and designs in the same spirit. . . . He has a reason for everything he does.[7]

[7]Eric [*sic*] Mendelsohn, *Letters of an Architect*, ed. Oskar Beyer (London, 1967), p 74; White, "Letters, 1903–1906," pp. 105, 107.

Wright told Wilhelm Miller that the "first important work which recognized artistically the influence of the prairie was, so far as I know, the Winslow house, designed in 1893"; see *Letters to Architects*, p. 51. A large prairie elm, Wright said elsewhere, suggested the massing of the house.

Wright first changed the roof and cornice, then the wall. He narrowed the upper wall and began to diminish the connection between wall and roof, support and load. The more he cantilevered the roof, the more it made the upper wall recede into shadow; and when he conceived the upper wall as a delicate frieze, the roof began to appear strangely free from support. In the Winslow house, the building from which he always dated his independent career, Wright already hinted at a dramatic horizontal rift between the upper wall and the roof [12]. The dynamics of the frieze and cantilevered roof above a "straight piece of wall" grew so central to his work as to inspire even his graphic designs [13].

But the problem of the confining wall persisted. Spencer wrote in 1900 that Wright was asking more from himself than "a masonry box full of rectangular holes." Isolated windows violated the integrity of the wall and paradoxically magnified the sense of separation of indoors from out. (Edward S. Morse had compared the traditional house of Japan to that in America and had described the latter as a "rectangular kennel, with necessary holes for light, and necessary holes to get in and out by." Much later, Wright wrote that architecture, so-called, had "chiefly consisted in healing over the edges of the curious collection of holes that had to be cut in walls for light and air and to permit the occupant to get in or out.")[8]

In the simple casement window Wright found the key for overcoming the confining wall [14]. An outswinging window provided both an unobstructed opening to the outdoors and an uninterrupted field for the geometric designs he so happily invented in leaded glass. The opened casement also became a small cantilever in answer to the majestic cantilever of the roof. But the casements reached their highest purpose only when grouped into a series, as a horizontally continuous light-screen [15]. Windows now composed much of the wall itself—a light-screen that took the place of the upper wall to form a splendid frieze of glass. This became a great victory, as Wright recalled, for architectural freedom:

> . . . the house walls were stopped at the second-story windowsill level to let the bedrooms come through above in a continuous window series below the broad eaves . . .. In this new house the wall was beginning to go as an impediment to outside light and air and beauty. Walls had been the great fact about the box in which holes had to be punched. It was still this conception of a wall-building which was with me when I designed the Winslow house. But after that my conception began to change.
>
> My sense of "wall" was no longer the side of a box. It was enclosure of space affording protection against storm or heat only when needed . . .. I was working away at the wall as a wall and bringing it towards the function of a screen . . ..[9]

---

[8]Spencer, "The Work of Frank Lloyd Wright," p. 67; Morse, *Japanese Homes*, p. 315; Wright, "In the Cause of Architecture," p. 157.

[9]Wright, *An Autobiography*, p. 141.

Above: **12.** The incipient rift. W. H. Winslow house in River Forest, Illinois, 1893–94. *Left:* **13.** Graphic design for cover of *Taliesin*, 1940. *Below:* **14.** Continuous casements. Playroom addition to the architect's house in Oak Park, 1895 (windows designed about 1908).

Opposite, top: **15.** The frieze of glass. K. C. DeRhodes house in South Bend, Indiana, 1906. *Opposite, bottom left:* **16.** Glass reflections. Robie house, living-room casements. *Opposite, bottom right:* **17.** Casements from indoors. Robie house, living room. *Above:* **18.** Structured vistas. Living room of Fallingwater, near Mill Run, Pennsylvania, 1935–37.

A continuous series of windows could protect interior space, and, if patterned with geometric designs in leaded glass, could guard privacy as well. Patterned glass gave great life to the frieze; the iridescent panes flickered with spots of brilliance, and the clear panes mirrored passing clouds and the flutter of foliage [16]. Indoors, the casements gained the rhythm of a folding screen [17]. As though to render landscape paintings superfluous, the casements gave definite pictorial structure to outward vistas [18]. Surely the frieze of glass had a higher purpose than "to let the bedrooms come through above." Bedrooms usually were minor spaces, the most private and indeed the last to call for more light or for broad vistas. When he fully understood what could be accomplished with a continuous series of casements, Wright raised the main floor to the story nearest the cantilevered roof, gave the principal rooms the most commanding vistas and, with great style, satisfied all at once the basic requirements of life: light, air and shelter. Such was one measure of his genius. But the overriding triumph of the light-screen was to set free the cantilevered roof. A great roof could not possibly depend on support from a translucent frieze of glass.

The new visual tension relied on a structural change he knew from having read Viollet-le-Duc. Small wonder, then, that in the 1910 Berlin portfolio of his work, Wright called for a revival of "the Gothic spirit." Gothic architecture, wrote Viollet, arose from the modernist spirit of its time to embark on a brave and uncharted course. Gothic builders, he said, were first of all concerned with the vault; they planned a building from the top down. The ground plan of a Gothic cathedral, moreover, revealed a remarkably changed ratio of open space to solid structure [19]. "Walls disappeared," Viollet wrote, "and became only screens, not supports." Wright saw that the cantilever suggested a system of support from isolated piers and short segments of wall. The wall could be further diversified through frequent turns and returns, and by narrow openings that effected vertical rifts. Hence the supports, moved inward and away from the salient corners, would no longer signify confining boundaries [20, 21]:

> The building now became a creation of interior-space in light. And as this sense of the interior space as the reality of the building began to work walls as walls fell away. The vanishing wall joined the disappearing cave. Enclosing screens and protecting features of architectural character took the place of the solid wall.

Centralized supports, Wright said, could "stand isolated, balancing load against load—seen not as walls at all, but as integral pattern . . . ." He exposed his sense of integral pattern in the ground plan, to which he now gave the sheer visual beauty of a musical score, making it not just a projection of the building-structure but a vibrant and many-voiced ornamental invention [22]. With such articulation he transformed the walls from ambient barriers into mere screens, companions to the light-screens.[10]

In pondering Wright's early work, Charles E. White, Jr., took note of the "huge brick piers, with glass and brick curtain walls between." But he completely missed the point: Most of the huge brick piers were not piers at all. They were only pierlike shapes that made a show of rising toward the roof and then stopping short of giving structural support [23]. An isolated or freestanding pier that carried nothing more than its own weight (or perhaps a large vessel for flowers) clearly presented a paradox. The massive pierlike shapes looked

[10]Wright, *Ausgeführte Bauten und Entwürfe*, p. 106; Viollet-le-Duc, "Construction," in *The Foundations of Architecture*, tr. K. D. Whitehead (New York, 1990), p. 165, and *Discourses on Architecture*, pp. 276–77; Wright, "Two Lectures on Architecture," p. 89; *A Testament*, p. 226.

Viollet's essay on construction was published as *Rational Building*, tr. G. M. Huss (New York, 1895).

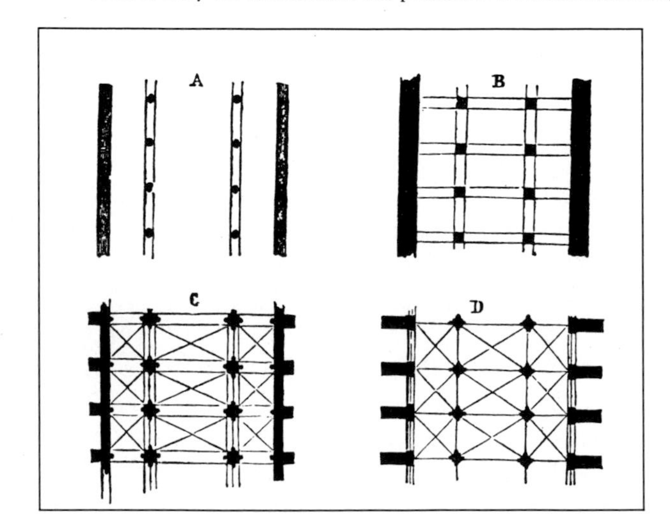

Left: **19.** From basilica to cathedral. Diagram by Viollet-le-Duc. *Opposite, top:* **20.** Isolated piers and short segments of wall. Detail from plan of Taliesin published in 1925. *Opposite, bottom:* **21.** Isolated piers. Fallingwater, living room.

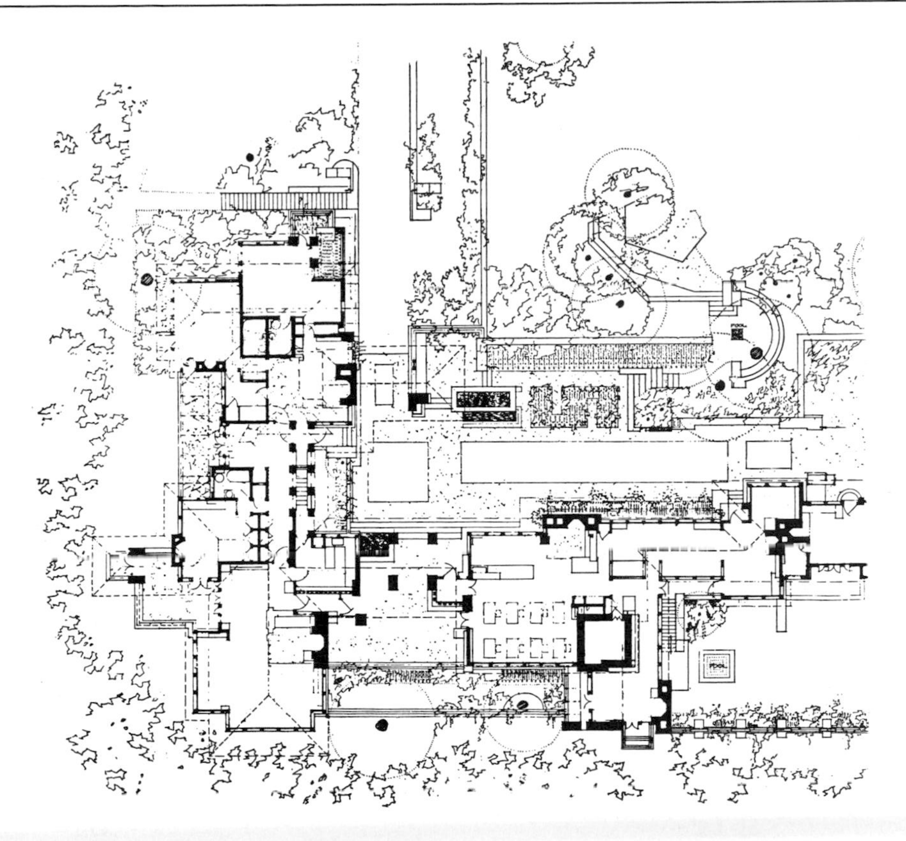

purposeful but served no literal purpose. Their mission was wholly expressive: to accentuate the thrust of the cantilevered roof by affirming its independence of the walls below [24]. Hence the pierlike shapes functioned as auxiliaries of a structural expression, the rift. To augment their effect, Wright sometimes moved them away from the building as if he meant them to secede; and to enlarge the rift near the extremities of the roof, he progressively reduced their height [25].[11]

Lift the lid to open a box, separate the sides to destroy it. For buildings with flat roofs, or roofs not visible from the ground, Wright devised further rifts in the vertical plane—narrow, rhythmic, unexpected breaches that conquered the confining wall by breaking it into screenlike segments [26]. As he released buildings from their prison of volumetric rooms, from spaces so predictable as to be grasped at first glance, he also ended the age-old opposition between space and mass. And from these new ways of conceiving a building, Wright could assert what seemed preposterous, that his Unity Temple had no walls. The

[11]White, "Letters, 1903–1906," p. 106.

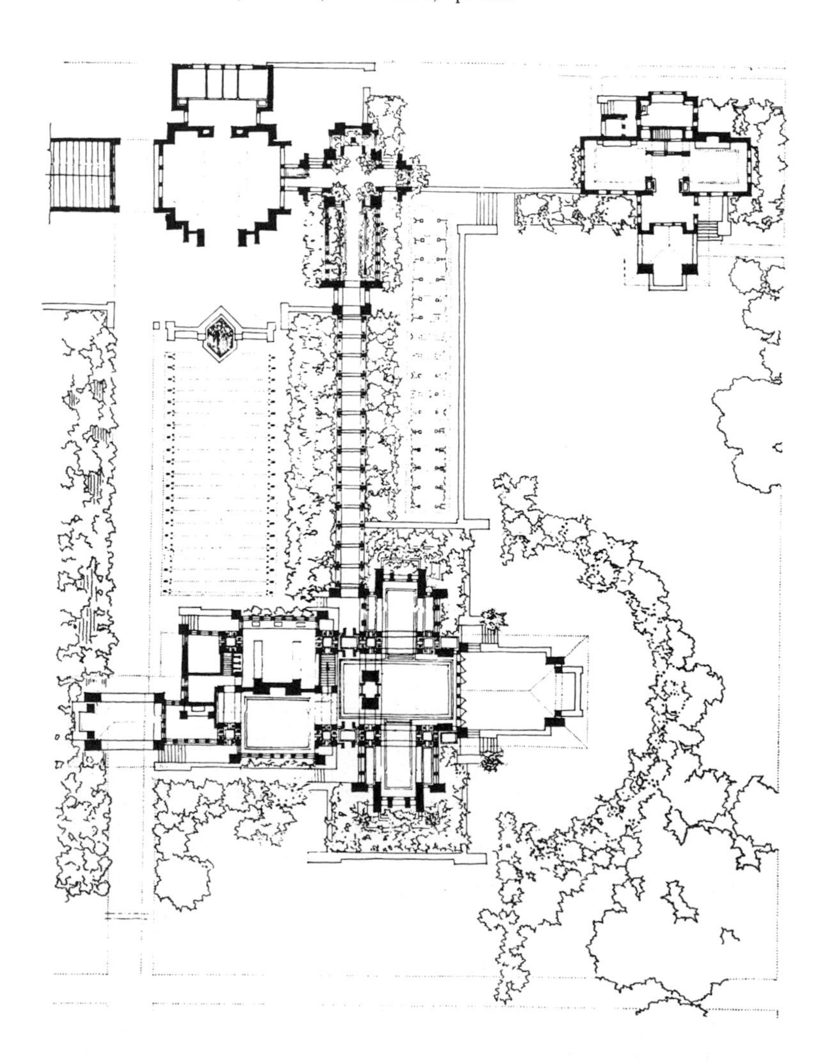

Left: **22.** The ornamental plan. Darwin D. Martin and George Barton houses, with ancillary buildings, Buffalo, New York, 1903–06. *Opposite, top:* **23.** Pierlike shapes. Susan Lawrence Dana house in Springfield, Illinois, 1902–04. *Opposite, bottom:* **24.** Pierlike shapes. F. F. Tomek house in Riverside, Illinois, 1905–06.

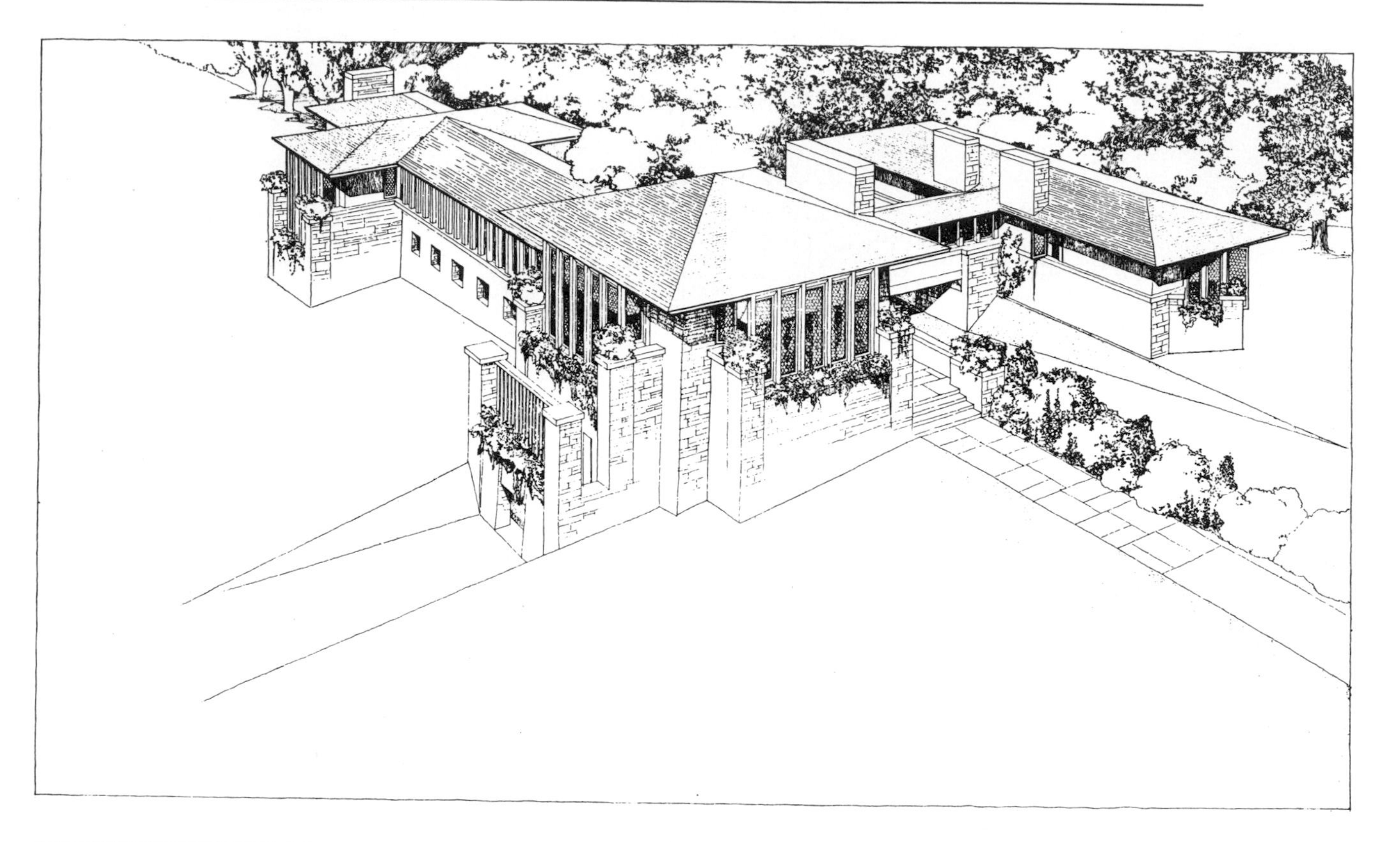

Above: **25.** Pierlike shapes. Hillside Home School, near Spring Green, Wisconsin, 1901–03.
Left: **26.** The diversified wall. Hollyhock House, Los Angeles, California, 1916–21.

idea of Unity Temple, he said, evolved from his struggle to articulate the Larkin Building, during which he revised the plan to make the corner stair towers break free:

> . . . I didn't know what was the matter. I was trying for something with some freedom that I hadn't got . . .. I took those four corners and I pulled them out away from the building, made them individual features, planted them. And there the thing began to appear . . .. I followed that up with Unity Temple where there were no walls of any kind, only features . . . screens grouped about interior space. And the thing that came to me by instinct in the Larkin Building began to come consciously in the Unity Temple. When I finished Unity Temple, I had it. I was conscious of the idea. I knew I had the beginning of a great thing, a great truth in architecture. And now architecture could be free.

Wright had shaped the stair towers of the Larkin Building as huge brick piers with little to support [27]. Thus the truly formative part of the building was not its central light court (a feature in common with many early office buildings), but a peculiar detail which goes almost unremarked: the channels two and a half feet wide, filled with fixed panes of glass separated by brick spandrels, that served to define the great stair towers [28]. Here were the vertical rifts that set free the corners, gave the Larkin Building its force of character, and, to Wright's mind, made it the "first emphatic protestant in architecture."[12]

More elegant rifts in leaded glass, only about half as wide as those of the Larkin Building, expressed the corner stair towers of Unity Temple [29–31]. At the top of the building, just above the frieze of glass, Wright cantilevered the roof five feet past its supports. He also pierced the roof with skylights (rifts of another kind) to give the auditorium the aura of a cloudless day [32]. Unity Temple looked formidable—like a mighty fortress, one could say—but its interior space broke free in every direction [33]. From the most static of shapes, the square ground plan, Wright raised a polyphonic complexity of quickened planes, a profusion of angles and corners, dissembled piers and darting strips of wood. Mass in effect disappeared. Unity Temple in those ways became a courageous salute to space and light; and Wright took pride in what he had achieved:

> The reality of the building is not in the four walls and roof but in the space enclosed by them to be lived in . . .. Unity Temple has no walls. Utilitarian features, the stair enclosures at the corners; low masonry screens carrying roof supports; the upper part of the structure on four sides a continuous window beneath the ceiling of the big room, the ceiling extending out over them to shelter them; the opening of this slab where it passed over the big room to let sunlight fall where deep shadow had been deemed "religious": these were to a great extent the means employed . . ..

The auditorium of Unity Temple confounded all expectations of the room as a simple

[12]*Frank Lloyd Wright: His Living Voice*, ed. B. B. Pfeiffer (Fresno, Calif., 1987), pp. 30–31; *An Autobiography*, p. 150.

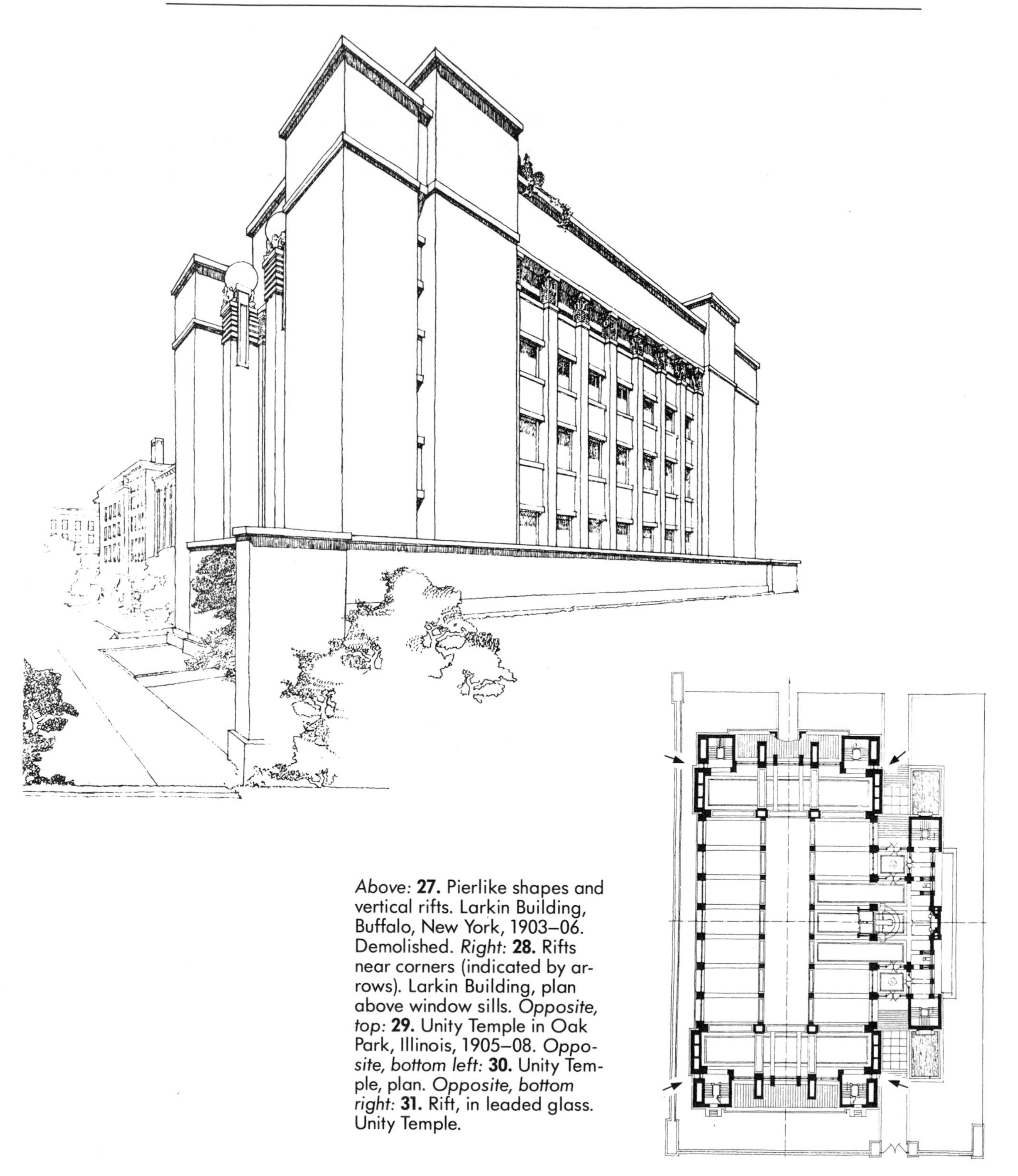

Above: **27.** Pierlike shapes and vertical rifts. Larkin Building, Buffalo, New York, 1903–06. Demolished. *Right:* **28.** Rifts near corners (indicated by arrows). Larkin Building, plan above window sills. *Opposite, top:* **29.** Unity Temple in Oak Park, Illinois, 1905–08. *Opposite, bottom left:* **30.** Unity Temple, plan. *Opposite, bottom right:* **31.** Rift, in leaded glass. Unity Temple.

FOR THE WORSHIP OF GO
AND THE SERVICE OF MA

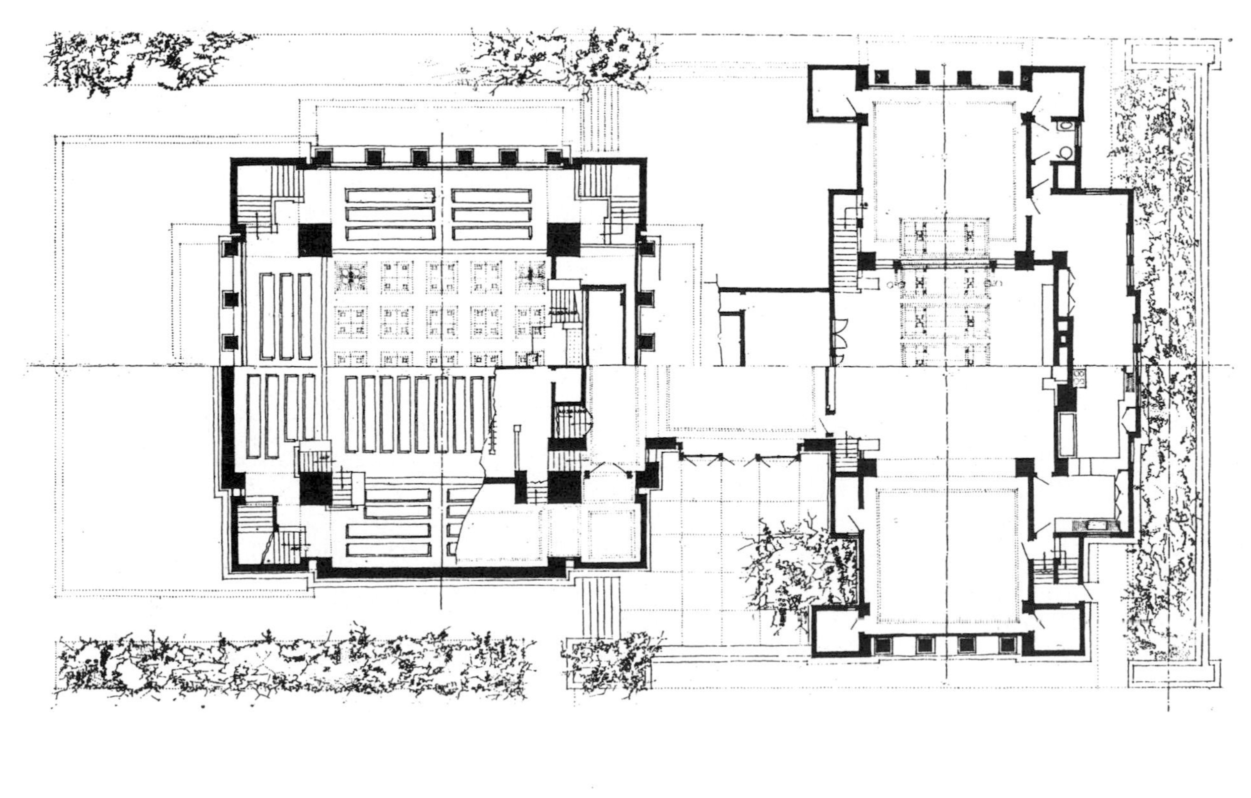

cubic container and inescapable impediment to the free spirit. Using the same principles he had put to work in imagining the "new shapes of shelter," Wright designed the interior as a perfect complement. Later, when he wrote of the Robie house in Chicago, which he conceived just as Unity Temple was being finished, he accurately spoke of the "organic relation between the exterior and the interior—clean, sweeping lines and low proportions preserving openness and airiness." An organic relation, because the outer form found complete concordance within [34, 35].[13]

By virtue of the same principles—the cantilever, the rift and the diversification of the wall—Wright realized all his highest flights of imagination. The same principles gave rise

[13]Wright, in the *Architectural Forum* 68 (January 1938), p. 35; *Ausgeführte Bauten und Entwürfe*, capt. to plate 37.

Significantly, when Wright wrote of the "continuous border of windows" at the ceiling of the high banking room in his City National Bank of 1908–10 in Mason City, Iowa, he observed: "These windows form a frieze of light . . .." See Robert E. McCoy, "Rock Crest/Rock Glen: Prairie Planning in Iowa," the *Prairie School Review*, vol. 5 (third quarter, 1968), p. 12.

After he traveled to America in 1911, the Dutch architect H. P. Berlage astutely remarked that Wright was working from the same principles in Unity Temple as in the Prairie houses.

Above: **32.** Rifts in the roof. Unity Temple. *Opposite:* **33.** The exploded room. Unity Temple, auditorium.

to his best buildings and projects, just as the same pattern of expression carried through countless details, even when they seemed eccentric. Wright could break open a cantilevered roof with a series of rifts or perforations to form a horizontal trellis [36, 37]. Two species of the rift thus might work in concert, one in the horizontal plane and the other in the vertical. Or he could rescue trees by letting them grow through special rifts in the roof or even the floor.

Indoors, he made ceilings the vital correlatives of the cantilevered roof:

> . . . the ceilings of the rooms could be brought down over on to the walls by way of the horizontal broad bands of plaster on the walls themselves above the windows and colored the same as the room-ceilings. This would bring ceiling-surface and color down to the very window tops. Ceilings thus expanded by way of the wall band above the windows gave generous overhead even to small rooms. The sense of the whole broadened, made plastic by this means.

Opposite: **34.** An organic relation. Robie house, view from the southwest. *Above:* **35.** Pierlike shapes, the treelike ceiling and details that reiterate the cantilever and rift. Robie house, dining room and breakfast alcove.

With long strips of stained wood—or what his eldest son Lloyd nicely described as stripe-moldings—Wright enlivened the shifting planes of the ceiling and created the effect of a broadly sheltering tree [38]:

> A most proper use of wood, now that we must economize, are these treatments using marking-bands or plastic-ribbons, defining, explaining, indicating, dividing, and relating plaster surfaces . . . . Architectural-articulation is assisted and sometimes had alone by means of the dividing lines of wood . . . the "trim" finally became only a single, flat, narrow horizontal wood-band running around the room, one at the top of the windows and doors and another next to the floors, both connected with narrow, vertical, thin wood-bands that were used to divide the wall-surfaces of the whole room smoothly and flatly into folded color planes. The trim merely completed the window and door openings in this same plastic sense.[14]

Ceiling lights usually suggested a leafy cover softly pierced by sunlight [39]. When he took the ceiling directly into the soffits of the cantilevered roof, Wright gave even more emphasis to the elementary planes of shelter [40]. If the roof was sloped, he still could establish the plane of horizontal continuity with interior decks for concealed lighting and for the gentle display of objects of art [41].

---

[14]Wright, *An Autobiography*, p. 143; "In the Cause of Architecture: The Meaning of Materials—Wood," the *Architectural Record* 63 (May 1928), p. 487; *Modern Architecture*, p. 73.

Opposite, left: **36.** Horizontal and vertical rifts. Guest suite at Fallingwater, 1939. *Opposite, right:* **37.** Trellis rifts, Alma Goetsch-Kathrine Winckler House, Okemos, Michigan, 1939–40. *Above:* **38.** The activated ceiling. Taliesin, living room.

Wright's purpose was always the same, to propel the spirit into the landscape. The cantilever, again, gave him a way to attack the persistent problem of solitary doors: their expression of an unwelcome separation of indoors from out. Now he could consign doors to places hidden in the shadows cast by cantilevered roofs, floor slabs, balconies or loggias. To approach the building was to be embraced by it long before one reached the entrance [42, 43]. He also fought the isolated door with a long series of French doors, which again he conceived as a great light-screen, not a mere puncturing of the wall [44]. In many of his building plans, telescoped wings diversified the wall by multiplying the angles and reentrants; but Wright's mastery of corners came mostly from the cantilever. Wotton said all "in lets of men and light" ought not to be by the corners since it was "a most essential solecism to weaken that part." Palladio had said the same:

Above, left: **39.** Dappled light. Fallingwater, bridge over driveway. *Above, right:* **40.** Ceiling into soffit. Samuel Freeman house in Los Angeles, 1923–25. *Opposite:* **41.** Interior decks. Taliesin, living room.

> The windows ought to be distant from the angles or corners of the building . . . because that part ought not to be opened and weakened, which is to keep the whole edifice upright and together.

Wright recognized that corners usually accentuated a sense of confinement:

> I soon realized that the corners of the box were not the economical or vital bearing points of structure. The main load of the usual building I saw was on the walls and so best supported at points some distance back from the corner. The spans were then reduced by cantileverage. So I took the corners out, put in glass instead . . . ..

Opposite, top: **42.** Delayed access. Taliesin, approach from the north. *Opposite, bottom:* **43.** Hidden doors. Taliesin, approach from the northwest; main entrance past fern garden. *Right:* **44.** The light-screen of French doors. Taliesin, guest room.

Glass by itself could have been enough, Wright said, to destroy the classical tradition root and branch. Glass made possible the rifts that defied confining enclosure by releasing the roof from the walls and by freeing the walls from each other. Even small openings to daylight could bring moments of wonder [45]. When glass met glass at corners, the effects could be breathtaking [46, 47]. "With corner windows all around," a client recalled, "the roof seemed to float above the walls." And that was exactly what Wright meant to accomplish.[15]

By extending parapets and garden walls deep into the landscape, Wright embraced outdoor space and gave it structure [48]. His best buildings expanded vigorously across the land, and his own country house Taliesin, in particular, not only seemed to be growing but literally had grown, from 1911 to 1959, through a continuing process of changes, rebuildings and wondrous refinements. "I began to see a building primarily not as a cave,"

---

[15]Wotton, *The Elements of Architecture*, pp. 52–53; Andrea Palladio, *The Four Books of Architecture* [1570], (Dover reprint, New York, 1965), p. 31; Wright, in the *Architectural Forum* 94 (January 1951), n. p.; *Modern Architecture*, p. 38; Herbert Jacobs, *Building with Frank Lloyd Wright* (San Francisco, 1978), p. 14.

Opposite: **45.** Unexpected openings. Taliesin, dining alcove. *Above:* **46.** Glass corners. Freeman house, living room. *Left:* **47.** Glass corners. Fallingwater, bedroom.

Wright recalled, "but as broad shelter in the open, related to vista; vista without and vista within." As to the vistas within, Spencer noted even in 1900 that Wright never lost sight of interior perspectives. This meant that the outward energies of the building, its spirit of organic growth, composed the prologue to a complex series of indoor vistas through which the interior declared itself an abstract landscape: refreshing, serene, complete and entirely comparable with the landscape outdoors [49]. With his rare talent for the seductively oblique, for the seemingly casual and soon to be slightly changed perspective, Wright accomplished in buildings the slow cadence of mystery and romance Jens Jensen hoped to conjure with nature paths that meandered past trees toward sun-openings [50]. If the goal essentially was the same—to create by the rhythmic ordering of space an air of expansive freedom—then surely the art of indoor landscape far exceeded that of the outdoor room.[16]

The sense and logic of the interior could unfold only through immediate and continuously changing experiences of space and light [51]. A building-plan on paper could never convey such richness. Hence the typical academic analysis of Wright's plans

[16]*Frank Lloyd Wright on Architecture*, p. 179; Spencer, "The Work of Frank Lloyd Wright," p. 67. In *Modern Architecture*, p. 59, Wright speaks of "this *unfolding* architecture as distinguished from *enfolding* architecture."

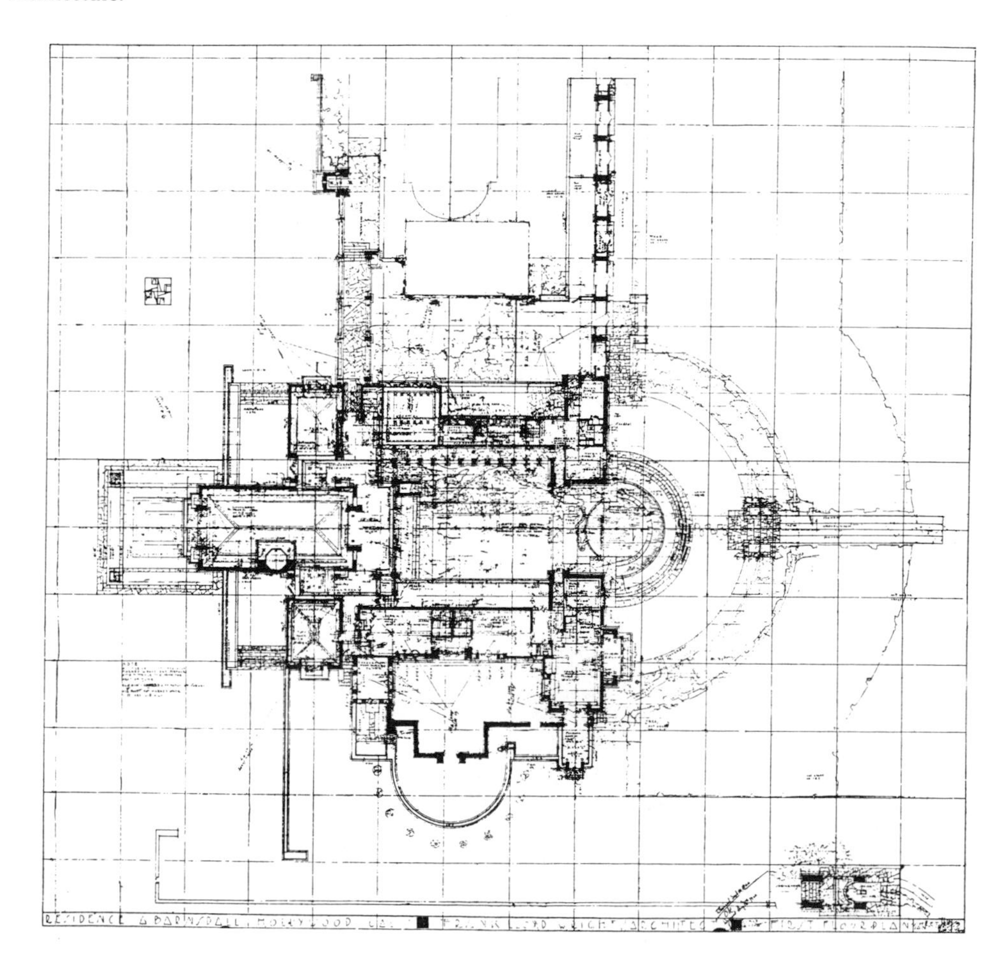

Opposite: **48.** Structure to outdoor space. Hollyhock House, plan. *Right:* **49.** Interior landscape. Avery Coonley house in Riverside, Illinois, 1907–08.

can reveal almost nothing about his architecture. Because the principles and patterns of expression in the outward aspect of the building prevailed inside as well, the interior spoke of the same equilibrium of deep protectiveness and vital projection into the open air [52, 53]. To shape the vistas within, Wright commanded an array of architectural devices: changes in floor plane and ceiling height, frequent turns, low and extended wall-screens, long casepieces, wood screens of stiles and rails, inglenooks, artful accents of flowers and sprays and perfectly placed items of sculpture or pottery, further pierlike shapes without structural function and, finally, frequent allusions to the cantilever and rift [54, 55]. He also hoped to design every piece of furniture as a child of the building, an epitome of its character. Furniture so utterly architectonic thus became powerfully expressive of the cantilever and rift [56, 57]. Chairs, tables and casepieces often came from the same mill as the sash and moldings:

> I tried to make my clients see that furniture and furnishings that were not built in as integral features of the building should be designed as attributes

> of whatever furniture *was* built in and should be seen as a minor part of the building itself even if detached or kept aside to be employed only on occasion.

Wright demanded from himself the same discipline in creating ornament. His earliest efforts were based too closely on plant forms, but he soon advanced to a more severe and inventive order of abstraction [58]. The goal was to conceive a grammar intrinsic to each building:

> In the main the ornamentation is wrought in the warp and woof of the structure. It is constitutional in the best sense and is felt in the conception of the ground plan. To elucidate this element in composition would mean a long story and perhaps a tedious one though to me it is the most fascinating phase of the work, involving the true poetry of conception.[17]

[17]Wright, *An Autobiography,* p. 145; "In the Cause of Architecture," p. 161. Also see Spencer, "The Work of Frank Lloyd Wright," p. 69.

In *An Organic Architecture* (London, 1939), p. 23, Wright says that the "furniture goes with the buildings—spawned by it [*sic*] really."

Opposite, top left: **50.** The outdoor room. Lincoln Memorial Garden at Springfield, Illinois, by Jens Jensen. *Opposite, top right:* **51.** Interior vista. Dana house, view toward library (below) and studio. *Opposite, bottom:* **52.** Shelter and projection. Taliesin, living room. *Above:* **53.** Projection and shelter. Fallingwater.

Opposite, top: **54.** Pierlike shapes. Dana house, stairwell near library. *Opposite, bottom:* **55.** Cantilever and rift. Robie house, living room. *Above:* **56.** Cantilever and rift. Table for F. W. Little house, 1912–14. *Below:* **57.** Cantilever and rift. Desk and chair for Johnson Wax Building, 1937–38.

"The most fascinating phase of the work" because to make a building complete and utterly consonant was to emulate the organic. If nature itself was conspicuously absent, as on "barren town lots devoid of tree or natural incident," he usually developed the ornament in richer detail. As his ornament began to reflect the shape of the ground plan, Wright made the plan more ornamental, a process both circular and self-reinforcing. Any motif could expect to resound throughout the building. Wright designed rugs, lamps, leaded-glass windows and doors, vessels, table scarves and table service as the ultimate flowering of the building process: a lyrical manifestation of structure as abstract melodic pattern. He wanted to give each building individual character and a wholly consistent language of form [59]. If that demanded an "interior discipline of voluntary sacrifice to an ideal," it was because he aimed at the highest level of harmony:

Opposite: **58.** Glass patterns. Dana house, stair landing. *Above:* **59.** The language of details. Dana house, living hall: andirons, fireguard and Teco vase designed by Wright.

> By now had come the discipline of a great ideal. There is no discipline, architectural or otherwise, so severe, but there is no discipline that yields such rich rewards in work, nor is there any discipline so safe and sure of results as this ideal of "internal order," the integration that is organic.[18]

Wright fought for the honor of an elementary truth: If architecture is the art of building, or *Baukunst*, then surely its products ought to be works of art.

[18]Wright, "In the Cause of Architecture," p. 157n; *An Autobiography*, p. 347; Wright, in the *Architectural Forum* 68 (January 1938), p. 100; *Genius and the Mobocracy*, p. 8; "Two Lectures on Architecture," p. 88.
He also speaks of the "ruthless but harmonious order I was taught to call nature"; see *Frank Lloyd Wright on Architecture*, p. 178.

"A NEW SENSE OF BUILDING ENTIRELY"

Frank Lloyd Wright pushed post-and-lintel structure beyond its traditional boundaries and toward what he described as "a new sense of building entirely." What happened in his work had not happened before and did not happen in the work of his contemporaries. The difference came from the fundamental shaping principles. Wright transformed the basis of classical architecture into an instrument for his thoroughly romantic imagination.[1]

To recapitulate: Wright found the architecture of his time to be a failed architecture, incoherent and an insult to the landscape. He advanced his own work only when he turned to an idea of the land and to aesthetic standards established by natural exemplars of organized form. He began at the roof, the elementary fact of shelter and its most poetic expression. From his feeling for the lost prairies he abstracted the lengthened horizontal as his dominant and recurring motif. To assert the horizontal by projecting the roof past the wall, he relied on the cantilever: his first formative principle. He divided the wall into horizontal zones, and experimented with a frieze that began to express a separation of the wall from the roof. When he changed the frieze into a continuous series of casements, or frieze of glass, he achieved a dramatic rift: his second formative principle. With the structural supports isolated and withdrawn from the perimeter of the roof, Wright heightened the visual tension between load and support by conceiving pierlike shapes that stopped short of serving any structural function. To increase the force of this rift he positioned further pierlike shapes at points farther removed from the building fabric and stepped them down and away from the extremities of the roof. He opened and activated the wall by dividing it with narrow vertical rifts into discrete segments, or wall-screens, by multiplying the angles and reentrants, and by staging the wall segments in sequential planes. The diversification of the wall became his third formative principle. Each phase of his development contributed to a vital expression of freedom that he sustained on a more intimate scale throughout the interior.

As he pursued a poetry of the horizontal, Wright took hold of such virile principles that he sometimes paid little attention to the particular landscape or specific site. This paradox he never quite acknowledged, even when he revived unexecuted designs to propose them for other sites, or made drawings before any site was secured. The primary,

[1]Wright, *A Testament*, p. 130. The so-called Prairie School followers of Wright copied the superficial details of his work without grasping its formative principles; their buildings typically lacked both the radical tension and profound equilibrium so characteristic of his.

60. The force of principle. Darwin D. Martin house.

independent fact about his art was always its unmistakable countenance of principle [60]. Thus the story he told of Mr. and Mrs. Avery Coonley, brief as it was, represented the central passage of *An Autobiography*, his major work in prose. A devout couple, they arrived at his Oak Park studio as enlightened clients for a large suburban villa:

> Mrs. Coonley said they had come because it seemed to them they saw in my houses "the countenance of principle." This was to me a great and sincere compliment. So I put my best into the Coonley house.

Mrs. Coonley's words resounded not only of the King James Bible, but curiously of what Wright himself had said a few years earlier of the Larkin Building, that it was good to "let the light of the Ideal outwardly shine in the countenance of an institution." By "countenance" Wright meant the aesthetic manifestation of character, and by "principle" the essence of character as the originating idea of form.[2]

Louis Sullivan had spoken of style as a quality that issued from a certain way of expressing an idea. Late in 1893, the year Wright left Adler & Sullivan to practice on his own, the partners received a letter from D. H. Burnham asking for a statement about their Transportation Building at the World's Columbian Exposition, then just ended. It was Sullivan who replied:

> We have sought to demonstrate in our work that the word style really implies first a *harmonious system of thinking*, second, an equally *harmonious manner of expressing the thought*. A system of thinking and the manner of expressing naturally require life-long study and cannot be special to any one structure. A thought to be expressed should, on the contrary, be special for each building and peculiar to that building.

Sullivan probably was paraphrasing Viollet-le-Duc, who said that in poetry there was the "thought or the impression" and then "the manner of expressing it." Viollet had defined style as nothing but "the natural savor or aroma of a principle" or as "*the manifestation of an ideal based on a principle*." The language of Wright's buildings continued to change, but the logic did not; once he had grasped the principles, his work no longer evolved. "Simple principles are alone productive," Viollet had said, and "the more simple they are, the more beautiful and varied are their ultimate results." Wright could hardly say more: Only principles, he wrote, would make of architecture something more than a mere matter of taste, and the value of any principle would be judged by its progeny. Because he projected the same ideas again and again, Wright found deep satisfaction at the end of his life:

> I am pleased by the thread of structural consistency I see inspiring the complete texture of the work revealed in my designs and plans, varied building for my American people over a long period of time: from the beginning—1893—to this time, 1957.[3]

So well established were the traditions of architectural structure that Ruskin in his celebrated chapter on "The Nature of Gothic" could say there existed only "three good architectures in the world, and there never can be more." Each good architecture, he wrote, corresponded to a simple method of covering a space, the original purpose of all building. Ruskin defined the principles as the lintel (or Greek), the round arch (Romanesque) and the gable (Gothic)—all of which he illustrated with a simple diagram [61]. The

---

[2]Wright, *An Autobiography*, p. 161; Jack Quinan, *Frank Lloyd Wright's Larkin Building* (Cambridge, Mass., 1987), p. 140.

Wright writes most succinctly about principle, character and form in *An Autobiography*, p. 233, and *A Testament*, pp. 103, 135.

[3]Sullivan, letter of November 11, 1893, in the Burnham Library, the Art Institute of Chicago; Viollet-le-Duc, *The Foundations of Architecture*, pp. 233; Viollet-le-Duc, *Discourses on Architecture*, p. 482; Wright, *Modern Architecture*, p. 61; *His Living Voice*, pp. 86, 101; *A Testament*, pp. 15, 16.

A, Greek : Architecture of the Lintel.
B, Romanesque : Architecture of the Round Arch.
C, Gothic : Architecture of the Gable.

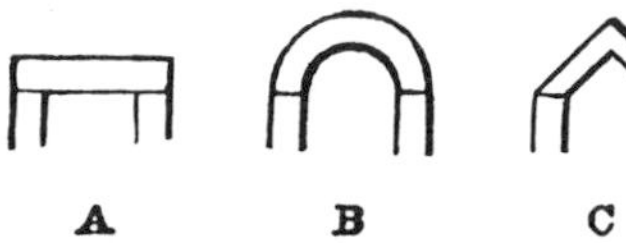

Top: **61.** "Three good architectures"; Ruskin's diagram. *Middle:* **62.** The lintel made large. Covered bridge over the Rogue River, Oregon. *Bottom:* **63.** Classical entablature.

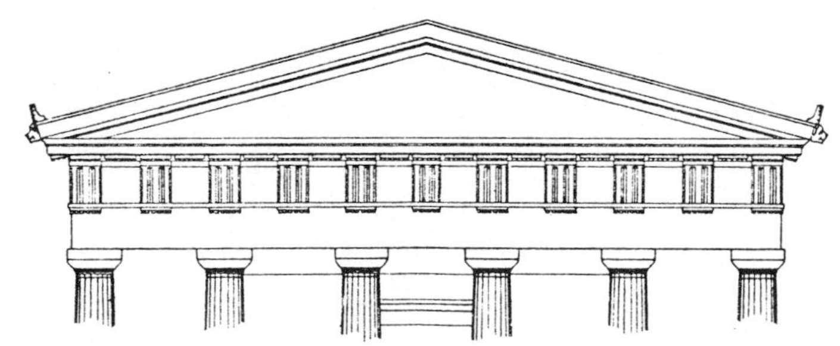

lintel degenerated during the Renaissance into effeminacy, he said, and it remained the least eligible principle.[4]

Yet the lintel persisted as an abiding basis of construction. Vernacular structures sometimes suggested a lintel made large, or even the elaboration of the lintel into the classical entablature of architrave, frieze and cornice, a scheme that inevitably reinforced and accentuated the horizontal [62, 63]. Wright could express the lintel with fresh simplicity, power and eloquence [64]. More important, he transposed the architrave, frieze and cornice into wall-screen, frieze of glass and cantilevered roof: an opened, enlivened entablature that rested not on columns but directly on the grand table of the prairie [65].

H. H. Richardson, whom Wright admired more than he could bring himself to say, already had combined a great sweep of the roof with a horizontal division of the wall that positioned very close to the roof a long row of windows [66]. The heavy lintels and sills nevertheless trapped the windows in place, just as the binding corners defeated an incipient thrust of the roof. Richardson usually conceived a building as a husk of hard and beautifully worked masonry in defense of an inner kernel of warmth and comfort [67].[5]

Sullivan, too, kept safely within the classical formulae of base, shaft and capital, of architrave, frieze and cornice [68]. Very much like Ruskin, he found in architecture only three principles, although he identified them as the pier, the lintel and the arch. The pier and lintel, Sullivan wrote, had brought architecture into being, but the arch offered "a wonder, a marvel, a miracle." The arch was the most subtle of the three principles, he

[4]Ruskin, *The Stones of Venice*, vol. 2, pp. 213–14. Wright too thought the Renaissance was a time of architectural degeneracy. "The artificial cornice, the column and entablature, become the common refuge of a growing impotence," he says in *Architecture and Modern Life*, p. 51. In his last manuscript, a projected children's book on architecture, he describes traditional architecture as trabeated (post-and-lintel), gabled or arched. See *Frank Lloyd Wright: The Crowning Decade*, ed. B. B. Pfeiffer (Fresno, Calif., 1989), p. 197.

[5]The complex and ambiguous relation of Wright's work to Richardson's is discussed by James F. O'Gorman in *H. H. Richardson* (Chicago, 1987), pp. 133–41 and in *Three American Architects* (Chicago, 1991), p. 120ff.

Opposite: **64.** The idea of the lintel. Hollyhock House, bridge. *Above, left:* **65.** Entablature on the prairie. Edwin H. Cheney house in Oak Park, Illinois, 1903–04. *Above, right:* **66.** Crane Memorial Library in Quincy, Massachusetts, 1880–82, by H. H. Richardson. *Below:* **67.** Crane Memorial Library, plan. *Right:* **68.** Wainwright Building in St. Louis, Missouri, 1890–92, by Adler & Sullivan.

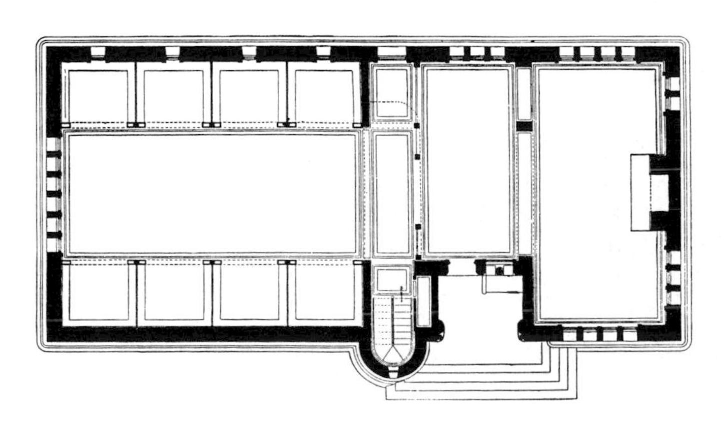

69. Cantilevers in nature.

said, and the most intricate, subjective and emotional. Oddly enough, Sullivan pronounced the lintel essentially unstable—an utterly stable beam would rest on the ground—but said nothing about the expressive potential of the cantilever. He saw himself as a nature-poet and yet failed to recognize the cantilever in every leaf, every outstretched arm [69]. When he responded to questions about the cantilever in an imaginary dialogue with a young man in architecture (who could just as well have been Wright), Sullivan took little care to conceal his contempt:

> Why have you said nothing concerning the cantilever?
>
> Because it is not primary. It belongs among those secondary structural forms which may be classed as expedients. It is neither one thing nor the other; neither pier, lintel nor arch, though it seems curiously to partake of their functions in a reverse or imitative way. It may assist pier, lintel and arch. Its essence is overhang . . ..
>
> What would the modern bridge engineer do without the cantilever?
>
> That is his business. What he does with it does not change its nature . . . he has raised the primitive cantilever to a position of high importance, but its nature remains unaltered . . .. It is our immediate business to deal with the art of architecture. So let us return to the road.

Sullivan once had regarded bridge-builders among his heroes, especially the chief engineers for the Eads Bridge of 1867–74 across the Mississippi River at St. Louis and for the Kentucky River Bridge of 1876–77 at Dixville. Strange to say, the first engineer used a technique known as cantilevering under backstays, and the second could claim to have built the earliest railroad cantilever bridge in America.[6]

Even the words "flying lever bridge," which appeared in an 1811 treatise on engineering, conveyed the dramatic nature of a structural principle that defied gravity to evoke the most daring of all events in space, flight. Bridge-building in fact would furnish much of the expertise for building the early Chicago skyscrapers, which transformed post-and-lintel construction into a fully integrated three-dimensional metal frame of slender skeletal members. Opposed though he was to the anonymous processes of modern industrial society, Ruskin discerned as early as 1849 that "the time is probably near when a new system of architectural laws will be developed, adapted entirely to metallic construction." By the time Wright was working for Adler & Sullivan, in 1888–93, skyscraper construction called on the cantilever for two special functions. To capture space-for-lease above the public sidewalks, cantilever beams projected towering bays several feet past building lines. Below ground, out of sight, cantilever girders protected the foundations of adjacent older buildings by transferring inward some of the loads of the new side walls, a procedure that inadvertently generated the first setback skyscraper.[7]

But so long as the architectural implications of the cantilever went unrecognized, the arch and the gable and the lintel reigned without much challenge. Wright himself experienced no wondrous moment of discovery; the erratic course of his early career makes that much clear. As he searched for what he wanted to express, he reverted too often to the arch. Favored by both Richardson and Sullivan, the arch remained a principle of undeniable grace and beauty. Yet it was inherently symmetrical, too easily self-fulfilling, too much at home in masonry construction. Charles E. White, Jr., described Wright's struggle:

> In this day of steel, he uses the arch very rarely and recognizes the lintel construction, by strong horizontal lines throughout the building. He is so adverse to the arch, that in a barrel-vaulted room, he usually tries to eradicate the effect of the sloping lines of the tympanum, by horizontal architectural lines in the decoration, or trim. He enjoys the soffit of the vault, but dislikes the tympanum.

An ambivalent regard for the arch in fact plagued Wright's entire career. In the vaulted playroom addition of 1895 to his Oak Park home he attacked the tympanum with a mural

---

[6]Sullivan, *Kindergarten Chats*, pp. 123–25; Sullivan, *The Autobiography of an Idea* [1924] (Dover reprint, New York, 1956), pp. 246–47. Also see Carl W. Condit, *American Building* (Chicago, 1968), pp. 144–46, 148–51.

Wright, too, was enthralled by bridges and once said that if he had not become an architect he would have wished to be a bridge engineer; see Edgar Tafel, *About Wright* (New York, 1993), p. 89.

[7]*The Compact Oxford English Dictionary* (New York, 1971), vol. 1, p. 81; Ruskin, *The Seven Lamps of Architecture*, p. 44; Dankmar Adler, "Light in Tall Office Buildings," *Engineering Magazine* IV (November 1892), p. 186. Also see my study *The Architecture of John Wellborn Root* (Baltimore, 1973), p. 137n, and essay on "The Setback Skyscraper City of 1891: An Unknown Essay by Louis H. Sullivan," *Journal of the Society of Architectural Historians* 29 (1970), pp. 181–87.

In *Light, Wind, and Structure* (Cambridge, Mass., 1990), p. 69, Robert Mark writes that ancient Roman structural development was "nowhere near so radical as that of the late nineteenth century, when the introduction of new industrial materials brought forth a true revolution in building design."

Above: **70.** The arch sprung free. Dana house, entrance. *Below:* **71.** The arch subverted. V. C. Morris Shop, San Francisco, 1948–49. *Opposite:* **72.** Experimentation. Dana house, south front.

in which the stratified wings of a curiously rectilinear genie sliced through the circular borders. At the entrance to the Dana house he made the outer curve of the arch leap past the abutments and made the inner curve jump to the midpoint [70]. He revised his drawings for the Larkin Building to remove an arch at the main entrance, but let stand an arched wagon entry at the rear. In the Wasmuth portfolio of 1910 he presented the Winslow house from a perspective that cleverly hid the arched porte-cochère; and he altered the front of the Hillside Home School by eliminating the arched entry to the cellar. In 1948 he sabotaged the telescoped arches of the Morris Shop in San Francisco by making the entrance an ornamental pseudo-vault that changed at the crown from bricks to glass [71]. And at the end of his life he conceived the Marin County Civic Center, north of San Francisco, as an attenuated series of superimposed arcades, a vast flutter of arches that were nothing more than pendant crescents, suspended sun-screens.[8]

The principles so characteristic of his best work came so slowly to Wright that in the elaborate Dana house he expressed all three "good architectures" at once and at the same time experimented with an intricate frieze and elegant pierlike shapes that established the independence of the roof [72]. As a compendium of all he then could do, the Dana house

[8]White, "Letters, 1903–1906," p. 106.

thus stood as a ripely transitional building. His practice had not yet caught up with the most advanced aspects of his thought. Wright had lectured in 1901 at Hull-House, in Chicago, on the painful discrepancy between the promise of machine technology and the dominance of old customs:

> The artist is emancipated to work his will with a rational freedom unknown to the laborious art of structural tradition—no longer tied to the meager unit of brick arch and stone lintel, nor hampered by the grammatical phrase of their making—but he cannot use his freedom.
>
> His tradition cannot think.
>
> He will not think.
>
> His scientific brother has put it to him before he is ready.[9]

What could surpass the meager unit of brick arch and stone lintel? High-strength steel and reinforced concrete would become the characteristic materials of twentieth-century construction. If neither existed in nature, both could claim a special nature—extraordinary strength under tension. Like glass, they could be considered everywhere "indigenous" and thus the most rational materials for modern buildling. Wright seized the paradox; he was amused to speak of "native forests of steel, concrete and glass." Steel and reinforced concrete, he said, promised a new freedom:

> Steel framing contributes a skeleton to be clothed with living flesh; reinforced concrete contributes the splay and cantilever and the continuous slab. These are several of the new elements in building which afford boundless new expressions in Architecture, as free, compared with post and lintel, as a winged bird compared to a tortoise, or an aeroplane compared with a truck.

As the agents of boundless new expressions, steel and reinforced concrete served quietly, their presence more often sensed than exposed. The structural skeleton needed to be clothed with living flesh because steel, despite its strength, remained vulnerable to rust and to the intense heat of fire; and reinforced concrete, although its steel was hidden, looked best when surfaced with smoothed and tinted cement. Honest construction did not demand naked structure, as Ruskin observed:

> The architect is not *bound* to exhibit structure; nor are we to complain of him for concealing it, any more than we should regret that the outer surfaces of the human frame conceal much of its anatomy; nevertheless, that building will generally be the noblest, which to an intelligent eye discovers the great secrets of its structure, as an animal form does . . . .

[9]Wright, "The Art and Craft of the Machine," p. 62.

This was the paradox. Wright gave form to space through a dynamic structural expression, not an exposition of bare structure. He was a romantic, not a mechanic.[10]

To the "new sense of building entirely" Wright brought a surprising mastery of the classical language of architecture, from which he knew that the post obliged to carry a heavy load also bore a palpable sense of burden. (Vitruvius wrote that the caryatid, a column shaped as a female figure, originally signified the punishment and humiliation of the women of Caryae, a city that betrayed Greece in the Persian Wars.) Even a small column burdened by a light load could deny the freedom Wright was after. Hence the import of an anecdote from the sculptor Richard Bock, who genially recalled how Wright changed a freestanding column by transforming it into two piers and a cantilever [73]:

[10]Wright, *Modern Architecture*, p. 96; *Frank Lloyd Wright: The Complete 1925 "Wendingen" Series* (Dover reprint, New York, 1992), p. 56; Ruskin, *The Seven Lamps of Architecture*, p. 40.

73. The column transformed. Fountain in Oak Park, Illinois, 1909 (replicated 1969), by Richard Bock with Frank Lloyd Wright.

Above: **74.** Piers and cantilever. Pettit Memorial Chapel in Belvidere, Illinois, 1905–07. *Below:* **75.** Piers and cantilever. Henry J. Allen house in Wichita, Kansas, 1915–18.

> At the time the Unity Temple was being built I was also commissioned to design a drinking fountain "for man and beast" in Oak Park . . . . My design was a center shaft with sculptured panels on each face, a flower box on top, and a trough-like base for horses and dogs to drink. I showed my design to Frank and asked how he liked it. He looked at it at length with approval, then he made a suggestion, took a pencil and poked a square hole through the center shaft, changing it to a double shaft. "Now, Dicky," he said, "you've got something." That is the way I completed it . . . .

The expression, of course, was one that Wright already had introduced in his buildings [74]. And he would continue to pursue it through variations and refinements, such as at the Allen house in Wichita, Kansas, where he attenuated the connection between the porte cochère roof and the brick piers below it by making the roof rest instead on paired cement blocks separated by hollow spaces [75].[11]

Wright always wanted the roof to look lighter, more free, the herald of a new and expansive American spirit. Thus it was ironic when European architects, well-grounded in the philosophy of architecture as well as that of nature, proved the more able to see what he was doing. H. P. Berlage saluted the leap of the "immensely projecting, slightly sloping roof" and said it demonstrated a "fascinating piquancy" of the three-dimensional. H. Th. Wijdeveld called the long expanse of roof an epic. Walter Curt Behrendt found parallels with nature:

> Here it becomes clear how the creative observation of nature turns into a new artistic vision. Take, for instance, the horizontal slabs boldly projected, that new motive which has been the most imitated in modern building: in these widely overhanging eaves, spreading themselves canopy-like over terraces and balconies, there seems to be plantlike existence translated into architectural form . . . . Notice the delicate relation between the building bulk and the detail: as the bulk rises higher from the ground it becomes looser and lighter, while the detail becomes more elaborate and more tenuous. Notice finally the new development of the roofs, which free themselves from the substructure through widely overhanging projections, and spread like lofty tree-tops, making the house with its loosened silhouette stand out against the horizon.[12]

---

[11]Vitruvius, *The Ten Books on Architecture* (Dover reprint, New York, 1960), p. 6; Richard W. Bock, *Memoirs of an American Artist*, ed. Dorathi Bock Pierre (Los Angeles, 1989), p. 90.

Wright had quickly mastered the classical language; see H. R. Hitchcock, "Frank Lloyd Wright and the 'Academic Tradition' of the Early Eighteen-Nineties," *Journal of the Warburg and Courtauld Institutes* 7 (1944), pp. 46–63.

[12]Berlage, in *The Complete 1925 "Wendingen" Series*, p. 82; Wijdeveld, *ibid.*, p. 3; Behrendt, *Modern Building* (New York, 1937), pp. 131–132.

Contrary to academic opinion, the expressive function of Wright's roof is opposite that of an enclosing element that "caps" the piers below it.

An architecture inspired by the repose of the broad horizon paradoxically came to express extreme structural tenuity. For the lengthened horizontal introduced a persistent ambiguity. The horizontal at ease with the ground produced what an encyclopedist once described as the "most complete and perfect notion that can be conceived of *stability*." If, however, the horizontal expressed lateral propulsive energy, it evoked the exhilaration of speed and the quickened rhythm of modern life. Wright always made the most of ambiguities:

> Clean lines—clean surfaces—clean purposes. As swift as you like, but clean as the flight of an arrow . . . to keep a grip upon the earth in use of the architectural planes parallel to Earth . . . .[13]

Because length has everything to do with tension—a beam twice as long becomes sixteen times more flexible—the exaggerated horizontal immediately implies a tensile system of construction. And because gravity strives to reduce any building to a mere mound of rubble, every building rises as a temporary triumph over dissolution. Nietzsche thus defined architecture as a victory over gravity, an eloquence of power in forms; and Schopenhauer declared the sole and constant theme of architecture to be load and

---

[13]Joseph Gwilt, *The Encyclopaedia of Architecture* [1867] (New York, 1982), p. 797; Wright, *Modern Architecture*, p. 35.

In *An Autobiography*, p. 146, Wright speaks of the arrival of a "New sense of repose in quiet streamline effects."

support, the aesthetic aim to make clear the conflict between gravity and rigidity. Wright's formative principles addressed the central challenge to any structure, that of sustaining loads across space; his exquisite manifestations of resistance to gravity went to the heart of architectural expression. Apart from the cantilever, the rift, the play of pierlike shapes, the diversification and the staging of the wall—all of which were intimately related to the contest between load and support—only an acute sense of gravity could account for so many of his expressive motifs. Spencer noted already in 1900 that Wright favored large urns "overflowing with flowers and dripping masses of foliage." Wright altered early photographs of his buildings by touching in hanging vines and trailing creepers, and in presentation drawings he added such subtle signs as pendant table scarves, little rugs draped over parapets, a fisherman's line cast from a bridge, or even a yo-yo spun from the spiral ramp of the Guggenheim Museum [76]. At the Kaufmann weekend house on Bear Run he made the plunge pool gently overflow in sympathy with the waterfalls below. Through such details he honored the force of gravity in the rhythms of growth and decay.[14]

It was also from an idea of the equilibrium of nature that Wright gained his understanding of a vital equilibrium in architecture, and how to resolve the paradox of

[14]Nietzsche, *Twilight of the Idols* [1889], in *The Portable Nietzsche*, ed. Walter Kaufmann (New York, 1954), p. 521; Schopenhauer, *The World as Will and Representation*, vol. 2 [1844] (Dover reprint, New York, 1966), pp. 411, 417; Spencer, "The Work of Frank Lloyd Wright," p. 65.

The process by which gravity operates remains a mystery. Wright once described the Larkin Building as a "genuine expression of power directly applied to purpose in architecture"; see the *National Cyclopaedia of American Biography*, vol. D (New York, 1934), p. 278.

Opposite: **76.** An acute sense of gravity. Perspective study for the Guggenheim Museum, New York, 1943–59. *Right:* **77.** The cantilever in holograph. *Below:* **78.** The cantilever in architecture. Kaufmann house, section.

Sincerely yours,

Frank Lloyd Wright

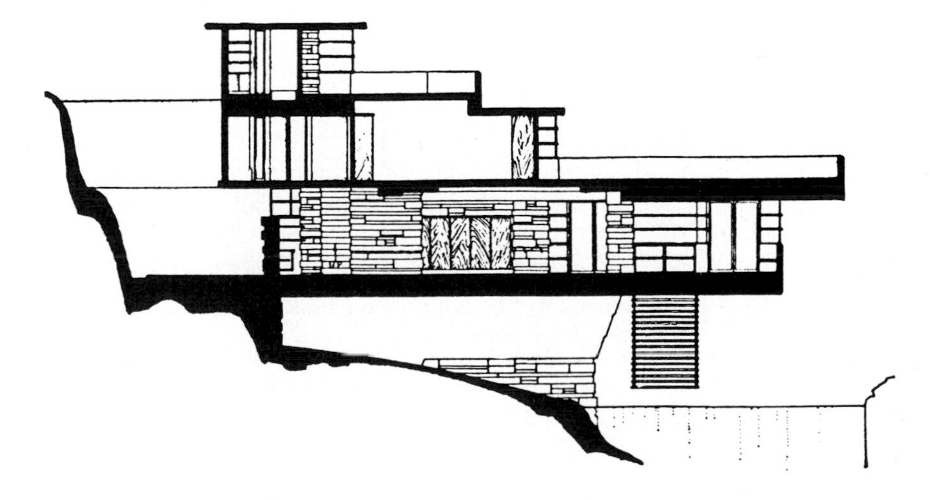

79. Shelter and freedom. Lowell Walter house near Quasqueton, Iowa, 1945–50.

simultaneous tension and repose. "Nature is never other than serene," he wrote, "even in a thunderstorm." He came to think like Heraclitus that nature's vast equilibrium probably coincided with the divinity. But there was also the example of the Gothic—its novel structural principle of equilibrium, Viollet-le-Duc had said, "almost transformed its constructions into living things." Ruskin, too, had remarked that the repose necessary for beauty was a repose "not of inanition, nor of luxury, nor of irresolution, but the repose of magnificent energy and being."[15]

The diagram of the three "good architectures" could not in fact claim to be final. Ruskin erred when he declared the lintel exhausted. By pursuing a romantic idea of the horizontal, Wright reinvigorated the lintel and changed it into the cantilever. "A new world of form opens inevitably with the appearance of the cantilever," he said. "It can do remarkable things to liberate space." Wright could have added to Ruskin's diagram a fourth figure, and it could have looked much like the shape he gave to his first initial [77]. Here was a perfect illustration of the energetic, open and free character of the cantilever; small wonder that it bore such similarity to the transverse section of the Kaufmann weekend house on Bear Run [78].[16]

All form, said Wright, was a matter of structure and consequence of principle. The arch, the gable and the lintel produced closed forms, opposed to the spirit of sunlight and the open air. Architecture could be something else entirely. If its reason for being was shelter, and its elementary content the conflict between gravity and rigidity, then purpose and theme became one when Wright manifested the equilibrium of load and support as a union of shelter with freedom [79].

---

[15]Wright, *A Testament*, p. 180; *An Autobiography*, p. 478; Viollet-le-Duc, *The Foundations of Architecture*, p. 259; Ruskin, *Modern Painters*, vol. 2 (London, 1846), p. 259.

In the *Architectural Forum* 94 (January 1951), n.p., Wright speaks of "Complete repose (especially in action)" and in the *Architectural Forum* 88 (January 1948), n. p., in reference to the Guggenheim Museum he writes of "this extraordinary quality of the complete repose known only in movement."

[16]Wright, *An Autobiography*, rev. edit. (New York, 1977), pp. 366–67.

THE COUNTENANCE OF PRINCIPLE

Once the form-logic of Frank Lloyd Wright's architecture is understood—and recognized as a constant—it casts a new light on his buildings and projects. At last they can be judged by definite criteria: the clarity, inventiveness, strength, harmony and grace with which they embody his principles. And the puzzling course of Wright's early career can be explained as evidence of his struggle to take hold of the principles and to put them into full play. His instinct for form sometimes outran his ideas, just as the ideas eventually shaped an ideal toward which his architecture would always aspire.

Two early buildings in homage to the prairie, the houses in Kankakee, Illinois, fell short of his mature expression because the gable roofs looked burdened by their own weight and because the extent of the wall surfaces below the eaves kept the roofs conjoined to their support [80, 81]. In the larger of the two, the Bradley house, Wright gave the living room a dazzling light-screen [82]. But the ceiling stripes still recalled Tudor beams—although they ran opposite the hidden framing members—and they countered any thrust outdoors. And even though the site offered a broad view to the south, and across the river, Wright oriented the house to the east and to a cul-de-sac.

The low hip roofs of the Thomas house in Oak Park, Illinois, sailed past the walls with a splendid confidence, but most of the casements timidly retreated from the corners [83, 84]. Curiously enough, the most dynamic part of the house was the breakfast alcove, or "demitasse" as Wright called it [85]. A nice way, at least, to begin the day. Just up the street, in the stalwart Heurtley house, Wright again elevated the principal rooms to the second story. The hip roof again projected far beyond the walls. Yet the effect of the masonry mass, of the strong corners and the round-arched entry, gave the house a ponderous and Richardsonian aspect.

In later years, Wright looked back to the Willits house in Highland Park, Illinois, as the "first great prairie house" [86]. For the living room and the master bedroom above he developed the Thomas house demitasse; but now it was the main roof that flared past the frieze of glass, and as the small supports withdrew into shadows, the corners disappeared [87]. The parapet of the front terrace protected the privacy of the living room and at the same time obscured the lower part of the light-screen, now composed of Dutch doors, so that it too could be seen as a frieze of glass. Wright had changed the terrace from a common amenity into a forceful expressive device—much as he would so many years later in the Kaufmann weekend house on Bear Run. Other roofs of the Willits house took flight at different heights to assert the expansive horizontal by commanding lateral extensions to the north, where the dining room gave indirectly to an open porch, and to

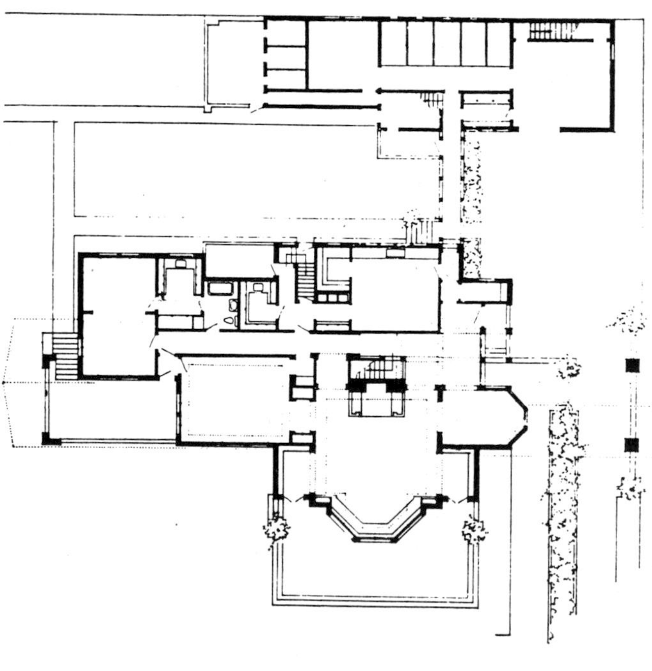

Opposite, top: **80.** Early homage to the prairie. B. Harley Bradley house in Kankakee, Illinois, 1900–01. *Opposite, bottom left:* **81.** Bradley house, plan. *Opposite, bottom right:* **82.** Bradley house, living room. *Above:* **83.** The hip roof. Frank Thomas house in Oak Park, Illinois, 1901–02. *Below, left:* **84.** Thomas house, first-floor plan. *Below, right:* **85.** The dynamic alcove. Thomas house, breakfast nook or "demitasse."

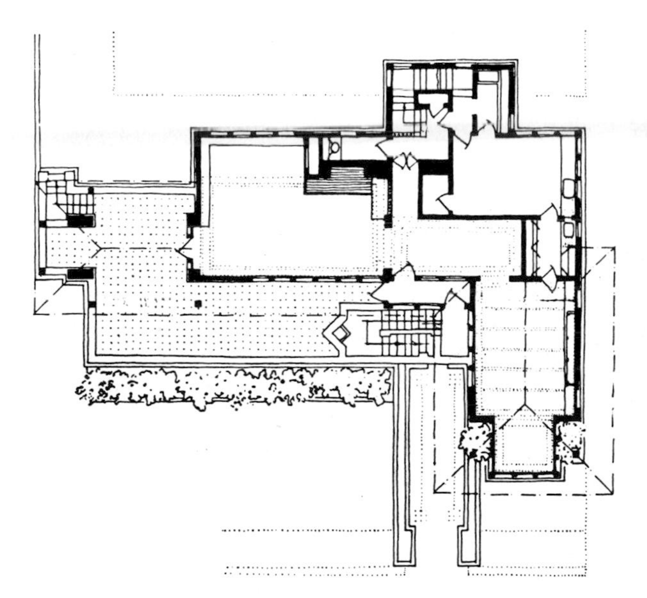

the south, where the reception rooms grew into a porte-cochère [88]. Flattened vessels for flowers accentuated the extremities and the cantilevers above. The plan, significantly, resembled that of the Bradley house, not that of the more progressive Thomas house. Wright advanced by new principles of expression, not innovations in plan.[1]

A few months earlier, Wright had designed for his aunts in Wisconsin a stone school

[1]Wright, *His Living Voice*, p. 27.

building near Spring Green. Its assembly hall stood as a beacon of the new architecture; the roof spread above great screens of glass, the pierlike shapes marched briskly away from carrying any burden, the corners broke free [89]. Inside, a cantilevered balcony on the plan of a rotated square sustained the dynamism [90]. Not long after the school, Wright designed the Cheney house in Oak Park [91, 92]. Although modest both in size and aspect, the house achieved such a paradigm of clarity and order that an architect of lesser powers surely would have remained content for many years to ring the changes. Wright, of course, preferred not to rein his imagination. Even for such a minor commission as the Yahara River Boathouse in Madison, Wisconsin, he projected a building of fresh simplicity and strength [93].

With the Coonley house in Riverside, Illinois, the Robie house in Chicago and his own home and studio near Spring Green, the years of Wright's great Prairie architecture reached their culmination. For each he invented an organism of individual character and integrity, and to none did he give an academic plan of the type so many historians have misunderstood as critical to his development. The smallest bore the most stern countenance of principle [94]. Challenged by a long, narrow, urban site with its principal exposure to the south, Wright reiterated the horizontal with an exuberance never to be

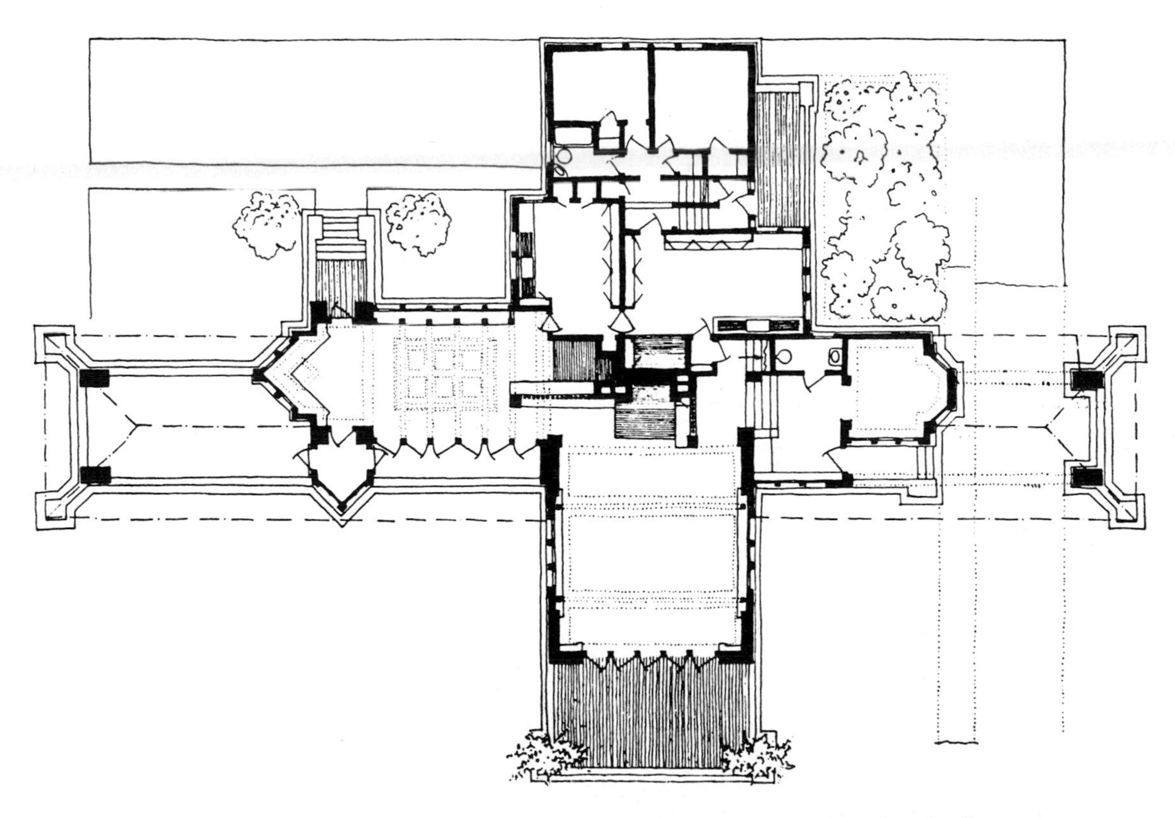

Opposite, top: **86.** Hymn to the prairie. Ward W. Willits house in Highland Park, Illinois, 1902–03. *Opposite, bottom:* **87.** The frieze of glass. Willits house, master bedroom above living room. *Above:* **88.** The expansive horizontal. Willits house, plan.

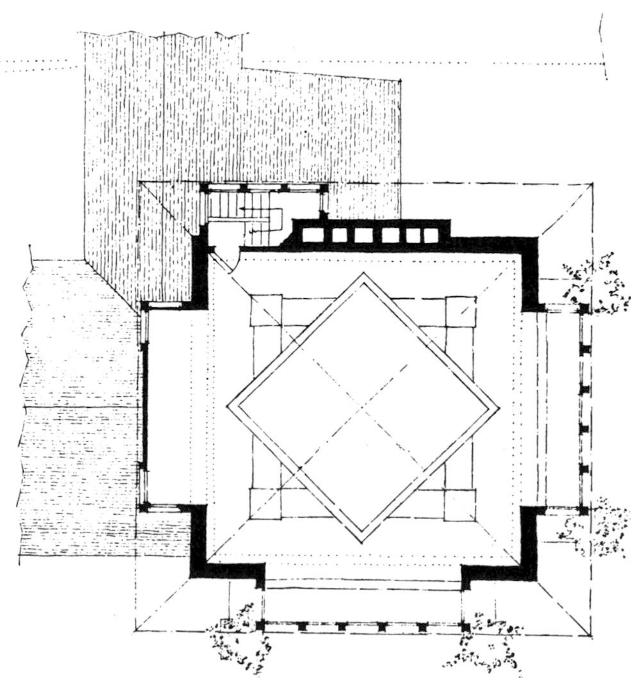

Above: **89.** Seceding pierlike shapes. Hillside Home School near Spring Green, Wisconsin, 1901–03. *Left:* **90.** Balcony plan, assembly hall, Hillside Home School. *Opposite, top:* **91.** The great roof above the frieze of glass. Cheney house. *Opposite, bottom:* **92.** Cheney house, plan.

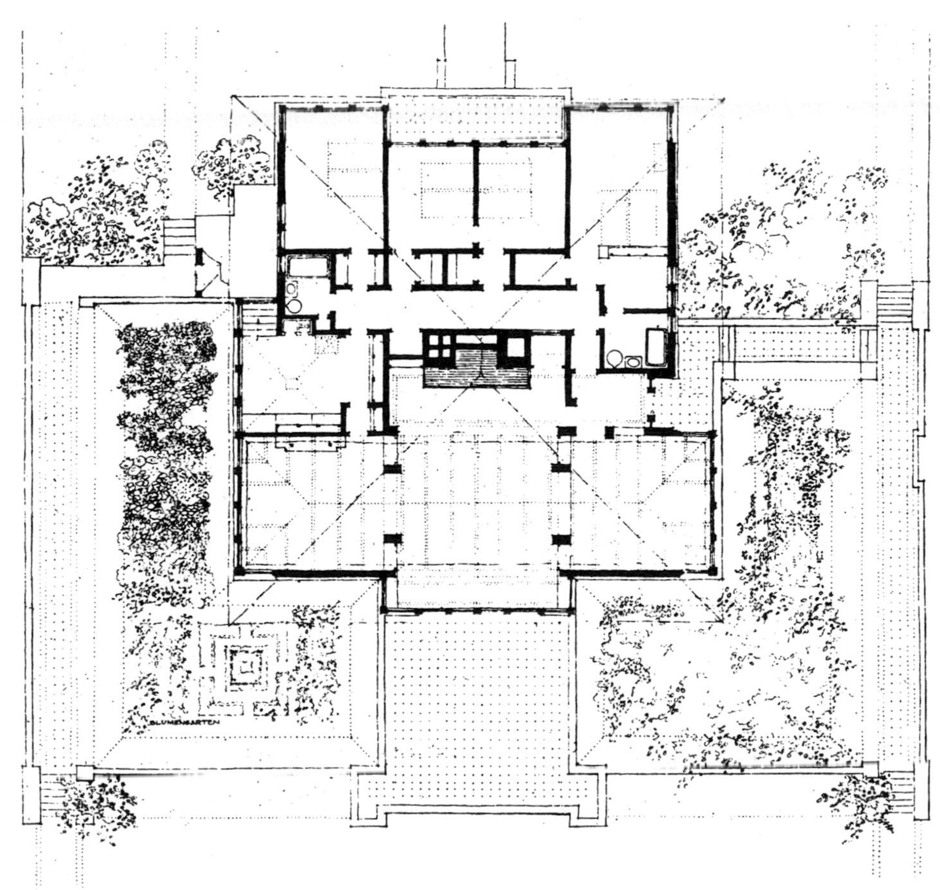
BLUMENGARTEN

Left: **93.** Yahara River Boathouse project, 1905. *Opposite, top:* **94.** Robie house, 1908–10. *Opposite, bottom:* **95.** Staging of the wall-screens. Robie house, west elevation.

surpassed. The long parapet of the south balcony gave him a way to express the continuous series of French doors as a frieze of glass just below the main roof. Small brick piers gave rhythm to much of the wall, and screens of nonbearing brickwork advanced to become the balcony parapet, court wall and south garden wall [95]. By staging the wall-screens and pierlike shapes in different planes, Wright created a pattern of delay, or foreplay, that enhanced and made more subtle any experience of the house. Streamlined vessels for flowers echoed the drama of cantilever and rift, and so did the courses of elongated bricks set with recessed mortar beds [see 111].[2]

After the prairie years and the tragedies in his personal life, Wright faced other landscapes, other climates and ways of life. He had designed an unremarkable house in Montecito, but the first California essay to which he gave his best effort was the Barnsdall house in east Hollywood, which he named Hollyhock House [96]. Here he conceived a much different countenance. The great variable in the Middle West had been the weather, its extremes of heat and cold, sun and storm, drought and rain. But in California the variable was desire: whether to be in the cool shade or outdoors in the sun. Given such mild temperatures and amiable oppositions, Wright found no compelling reason to express the roof as the agent of shelter. The roofs of Hollyhock House thus served as elevated terraces or promenades that provided vistas in all directions [97]. Lingering vestiges of the cantilever and rift appeared in the porte-cochère and bedroom wing, but narrow vertical rifts best expressed the freedom of the building by opening and dividing

[2]Also see my study, *Frank Lloyd Wright's Robie House* (Dover, New York, 1984).

Opposite, top: **96.** A new countenance for the West. Study for Hollyhock House, 1916–21. *Opposite, bottom:* **97.** Outward vistas. Hollyhock House. *Right:* **98.** Wall rift. Hollyhock House. *Below:* **99.** Hollyhock House, garden court.

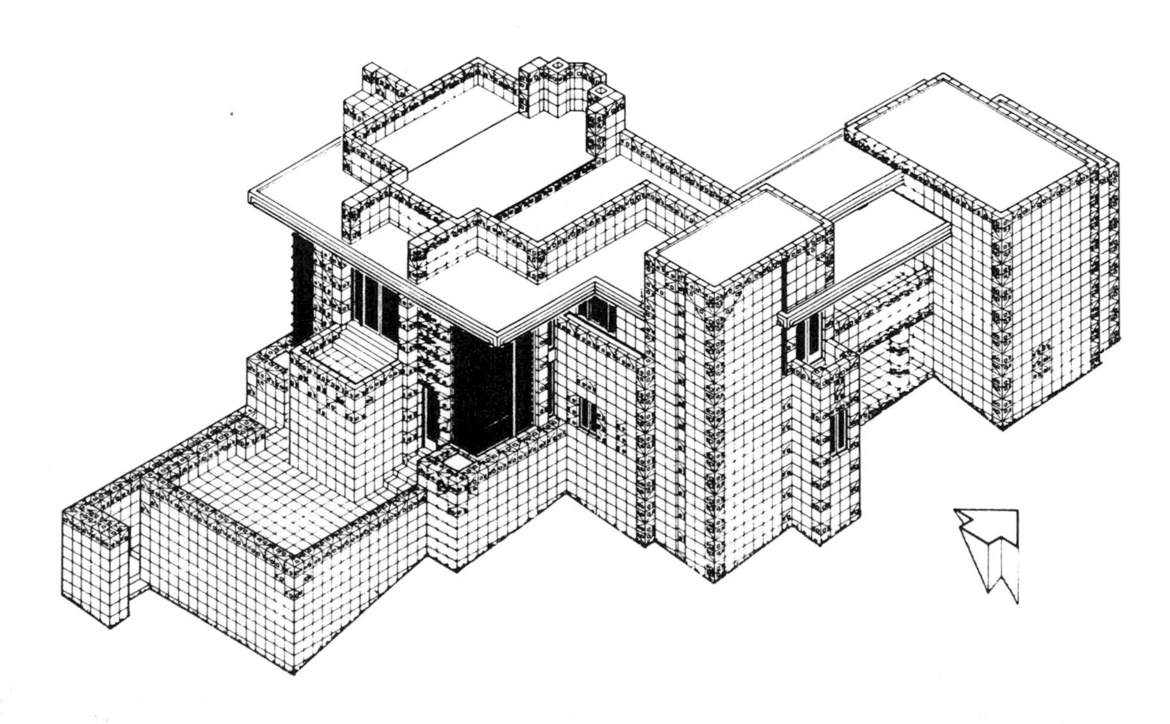

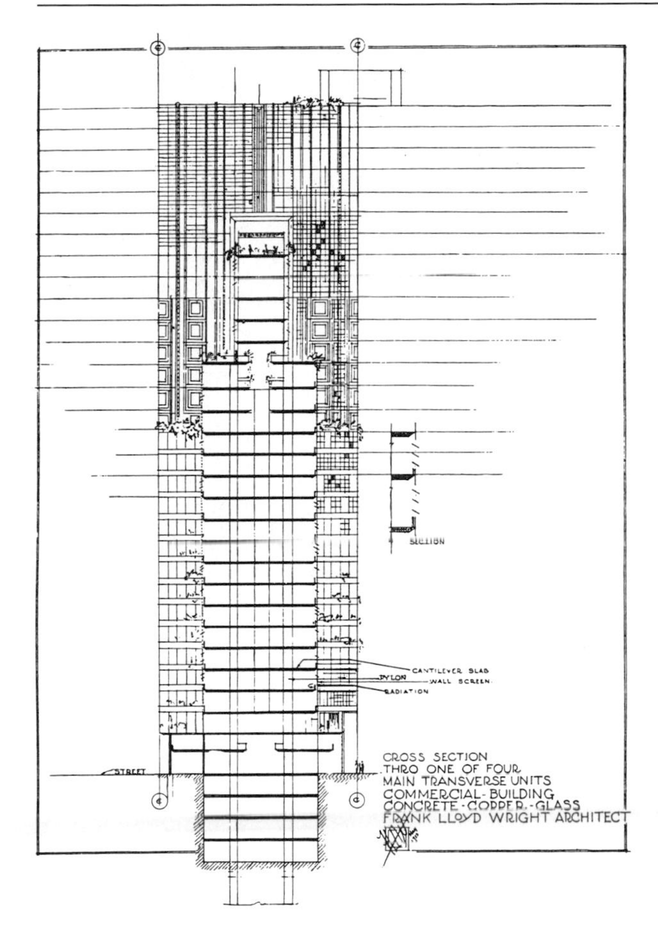

Opposite, top: **100.** Wall rifts. Freeman house, 1923–25. *Opposite, bottom:* **101.** Cellular structure. Freeman house. *Left:* **102.** Cantilever office tower. Project, 1923–24.

the wall into segments as beautifully proportioned as folding screens or hanging scroll-paintings [98]. And the central garden court was open to the sky [99].[3]

In the California houses he built of concrete blocks cast from special molds, Wright sometimes perforated the walls in sprightly abstract patterns, rifts of still another kind [100]. This changed the wall-screen into a sun-screen. Because structure and ornament now became one, the block houses reached a new relation to the organic. They emulated living creatures with muscles and skin formed alike of cellular tissue [101]. Although the cantilever principle seemed in retreat, it shortly reappeared with redoubled vigor. As a response to what he considered "the skyscraper problem," Wright proposed a cantilever glass office tower in which reinforced-concrete floor slabs projected well beyond the interior concrete pylons [102]. The entire construction, he said, would be "balanced as the body on the legs, the walls hanging as the arms from the shoulders." The outer wall-screen, formed of glass within a matrix of sheet copper, would become a colossal light-screen.[4]

---

[3]Also see my study, *Frank Lloyd Wright's Hollyhock House* (Dover, New York, 1992).

[4]Wright, "In the Cause of Architecture—Sheet Metal and a Modern Instance," the *Architectural Record* 64 (October 1928), pp. 338–42; *An Autobiography*, p. 258.

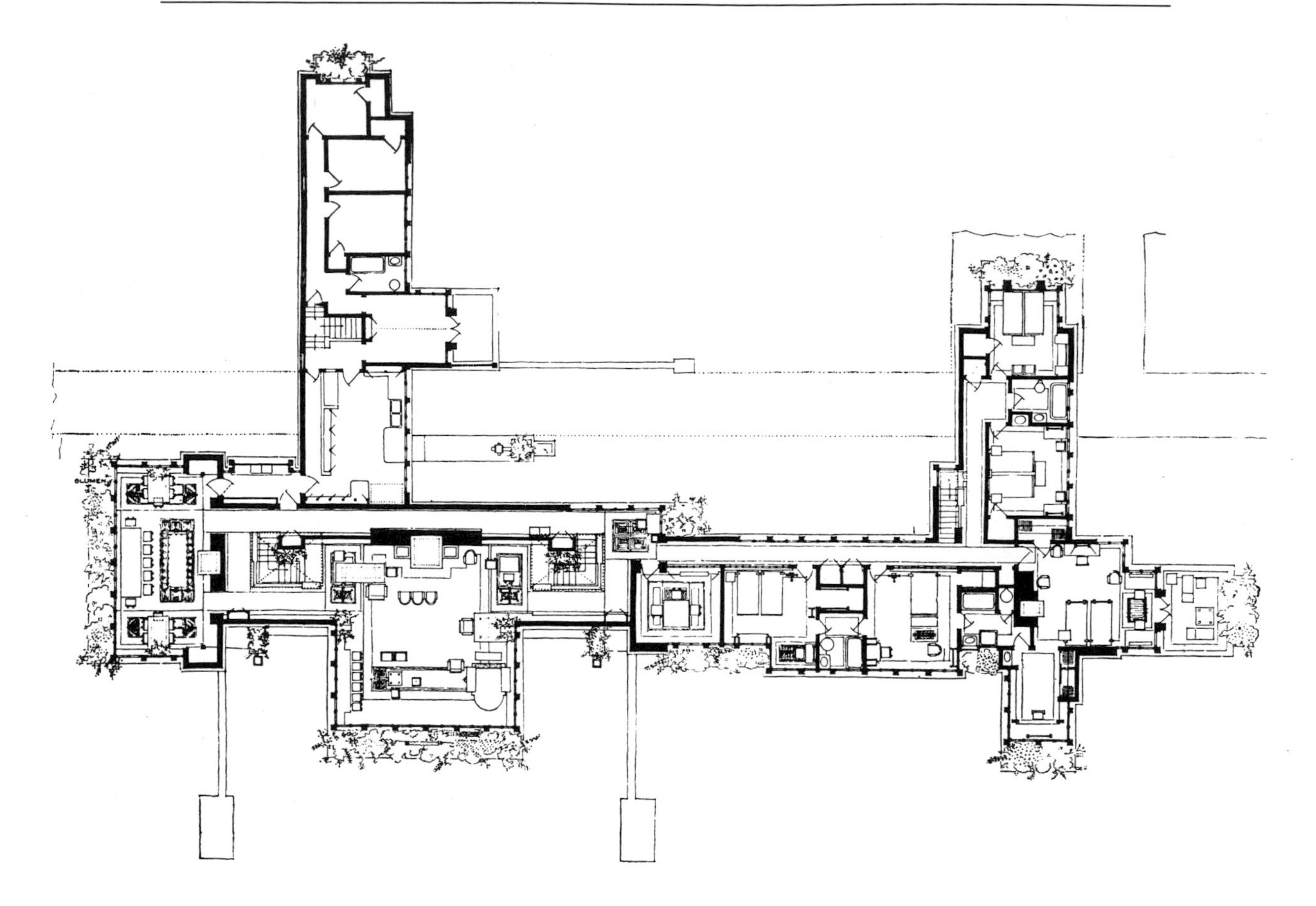

The lean years had begun for Wright long before the Depression, but the 1930s turned him again to the house of moderate size and cost—and the problem of how to give it style and a sense of expanding freedom. As early as 1896, he had written that the private house represented the central building type in American democratic life and had "a far more intimate influence on spiritual growth and physical well-being than cathedrals and palaces." Now he proposed what he named the Usonian house, variants of which he produced for the rest of his life. His idea of a lengthened and basically single-story house with the living spaces well segregated from those for sleeping had appeared much earlier, and notably in the Coonley house [103]. Hence the Usonian house was a simplified and somewhat diluted prairie house characterized by an absence of leaded glass and the presence of a concrete floor-mat, of gravity heating from small pipes below the floor, and a system of very thin wall-screens with a striated effect from wide boards spaced by recessed battens. The typical Usonian had far more flair and snap than the familiar ranch house [104]. Isolated brick piers countered the waferlike walls, the interior spaces conversed poetically with light and, although the oblique vistas were now less defined and less evocative, they still had charm. Yet the Usonians lacked the intensity of discipline and detail in the best of the Prairie houses. The glass doors from floor to ceiling addressed the open air with neither the dynamics nor the subtlety of the frieze of glass. The narrow

Opposite: **103.** Coonley house, plan. *Above:* **104.** Goetsch-Winckler house, 1939–40. *Left:* **105.** Stanley Rosenbaum house in Florence, Alabama, 1939–40, living room.

Above: **106.** Carport and cantilever. Herbert Jacobs house in Madison, Wisconsin, 1936–37. *Below:* **107.** Fallingwater, 1935–37. *Opposite:* **108.** Projecting ledges. Rock structure on Bear Run.

clerestories and ceiling lights, sometimes ornamented by meager perforated boards, became pale descendants of the rifts of old. So far as the cantilever, however, the Usonians played a gallant role. Wright had pondered how much he could trim from construction costs; he declared pitched roofs "expensive and unnecessary." The flat roof gave a bolder expression to the cantilever and especially to the continuity of indoor ceiling with outdoor soffit [105]. To eliminate the expense of a garage, Wright devised what he named the *carport*, essentially a porte-cochère streamlined and changed into a cul-de-sac [106]. It, too, offered fresh opportunities for the dramatic cantilever.[5]

In the midst of the Depression, astonishingly, Wright accomplished two great buildings. One of them quickly became the most celebrated of his entire career [107]. Conceived as a weekend house poised above the waterfalls of an obscure mountain stream, Fallingwater stands as both the consummate manifesto of all his principles and as an apotheosis of the contest between gravity and rigidity. Although he meant to honor the forest site, Wright also chose to compete with the high drama of the falls and with the insistent asymmetric rhythms of the projecting sandstone ledges and long cantilevered leaves [108]. "Cantilever slabs overhanging each other leaping out from the rock ledge behind," he wrote of the house as it was being completed:

[5]Wright, "Architect, Architecture, and the Client" [1896], in *Collected Writings*, vol. 1, p. 29; *An Autobiography*, p. 491.

Wright deplored the usual garage as a "gaping hole"; see *Frank Lloyd Wright on Architecture*, p. 203. Also see John Sergeant, *Frank Lloyd Wright's Usonian Houses* (New York, 1976).

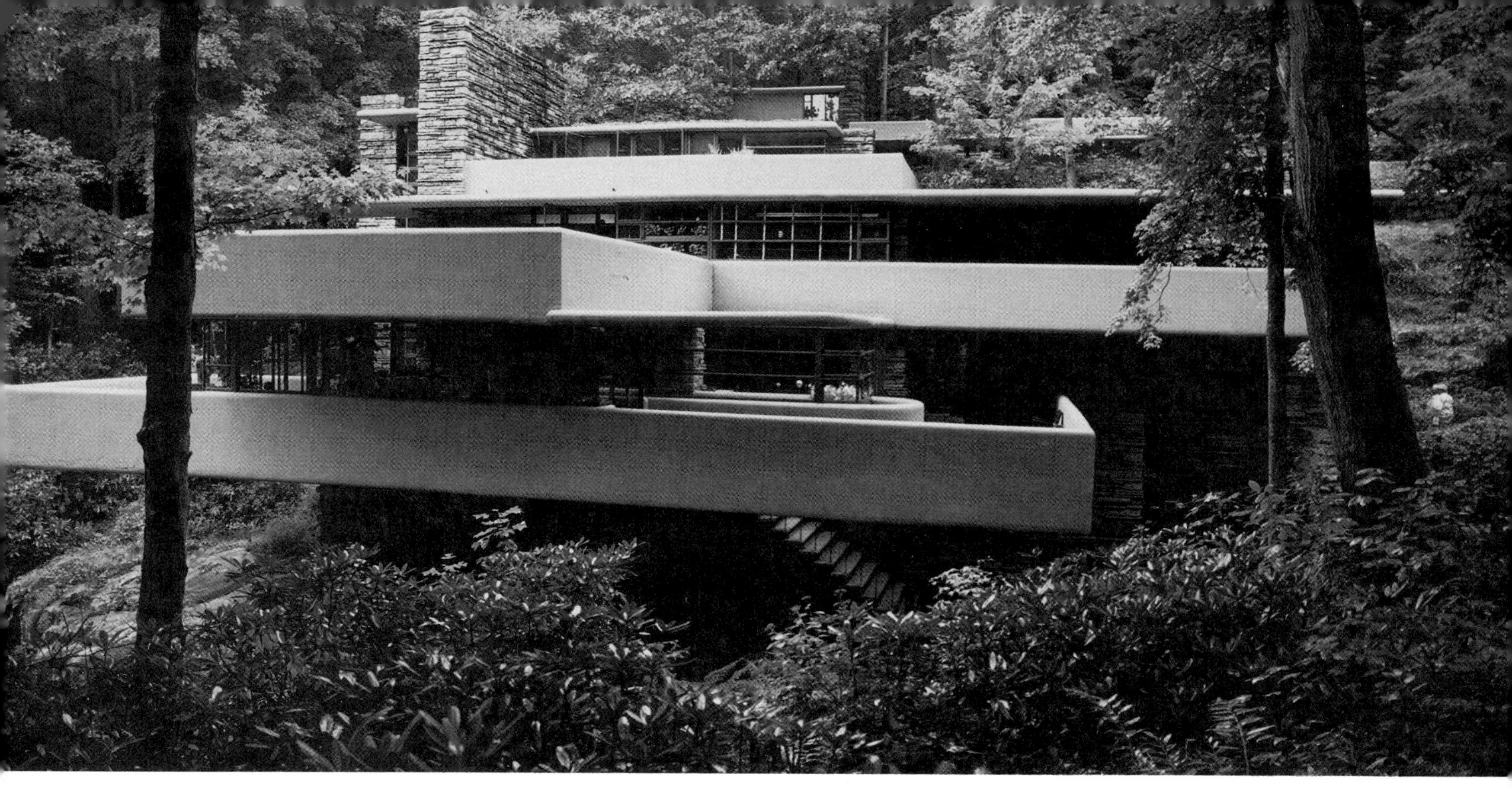

Above: **109.** Fallingwater, from the southeast. *Below:* **110.** Robie house, from the southeast.

> For the first time in my practice, where residence work is concerned in recent years, reenforced concrete was actually needed to construct the cantilever system of this extension of the cliff beside a mountain stream, making living space over and above the stream upon several terraces upon which a man who loved the place sincerely, one who liked to listen to the waterfall, might well live. Steel sash came within reach also for the first time. In this design for living down in a glen in a deep forest, shelter took on definite masonry form while still preserving protection overhead for extensive glass surface . . ..
>
> This structure might serve to indicate that the sense of shelter—the sense of space where used with sound structural sense—has no limitations as to form except the materials used and the methods by which they are employed for what purpose. The ideas involved here are in no wise changed from those of early work. The materials and methods of construction come through them, here, as they may and will always come through everywhere. That is all. The effects you see in this house are not superficial effects.[6]

Wright intended to refute his critics and all apologists for the International Style—which he scorned as a shallow, secondhand modernism. As early as 1894 he had spoken against the boxlike house that looked "as though it had been cut from cardboard with a pair of scissors and whitewashed for luck." The effects of Fallingwater, he asserted, proved "entirely consistent with the prairie houses of 1901–10." And so they did. Plain to see, the south face of Fallingwater and the south face of the Robie house issued from the same principles, the same imagination [109, 110]. The details, too, were shaped by the same ideas. Just as the long narrow bricks of the Robie house repeated the fleeting horizontals of the entire building, the finest stonework at Bear Run could evoke swiftly passing sticks in the stream, the ceaseless flux that Heraclitus found at the heart of life [111, 112].[7]

The house on Bear Run defied every expectation. It refused to step lightly down the hill in deference to the waterfalls, and it imposed grand horizontals on a precipitously vertical site. It deliberately obscured many points of view toward the falls, only to deflect attention to the monotonous sound of the water. And although the house appeared serene from some perspectives, it remained an intruder in the forest. At close range, moreover, it revealed its great struggle to sustain a precarious equilibrium. Costly to construct and even more costly to keep up, Fallingwater was built of so much reinforced concrete and so much steel sash it could not begin to pass for the simple weekend retreat the clients had originally proposed [113]. In short, Fallingwater flouted all the rules. A great imagination advanced

---

[6]Wright, in the *Architectural Forum* 68 (January 1938), pp. 41, 36.

[7]Wright, "The Architect and the Machine," p. 21; *Frank Lloyd Wright on Architecture*, p. 232.
He praises Heraclitus in *An Organic Architecture*, p. 45, and in *Architecture and Modern Life*, p. 19, declares: "Change is the one immutable circumstance found in landscape." Fallingwater is immensely more significant as a summation of Wright's art than as a polemic against the International Style.

Opposite, top left: **111.** Robie house, brickwork. *Opposite, top right:* **112.** Fallingwater, stonework. *Opposite, bottom:* **113.** Concrete, steel and glass. Fallingwater, reading alcove. *Right:* **114.** Rifts in every plane. Fallingwater, skylight, hatch to stream and doors to terrace. *Below:* **115.** Terraces of living space. Fallingwater, from the east.

freedom by going where none had gone before. Fallingwater overcame every plane of confinement: the wall, the ceiling, even the floor [114]. Wright put cantilevers to work in five of the six terraces, which altogether offered nearly as much floor space as the entire interior. If deprived of its terraces, Fallingwater would also lose its essence [115]. The terraces and roofs generated the shadowed horizontal rifts that echoed the rift in the rock at the falls. The vertical rifts reached a climax in the light-screen of the kitchen and west

bedrooms, a three-story tower of glass between the west wall and the stone chimney mass, which answered the falls as an abstract cascade. Narrow rifts from floor to ceiling acted almost alone to articulate the walls of the servants' wing and guest quarters, but Wright diversified the walls of the main house into scattered segments [116]. Fallingwater was a house without four walls. It had nine [117].[8]

Less than a year later, for an urban site that lacked vistas of any interest, Wright planned the Johnson Wax Building without windows [118]. How could it speak of freedom? The cantilever and rift now separated the walls from the roof in a most radical

[8]Also see my study, *Frank Lloyd Wright's Fallingwater,* rev. edit. (Dover, New York, 1993).

way. Just where the eye expected the building to come together, Wright inserted a horizontal band of glass tubes. This "open glass-filled rift," he wrote, supplanted the hallowed cornice:

> I came upon the elimination of the horizontal corner, the corner between the walls and ceiling . . . . Architecture (until then) was finally closed off at the upper angle by the heavy artillery called a cornice. This time . . . I took off the cornice at the ceiling, took out the wall beneath it and so in this sacrosanct region I put in glass. Thus light was let into the interior space where light had never been seen before.

The glass-filled rift (or "clerestory sunband," as Wright sometimes described it) changed the brick walls into mere screens [119]. The roof now rested on a grid of interior cantilevers—circular pads that spread from a grove of concrete columns [120]. Wright called the columns "hollow slender monolithic dendriform shafts or stems." They stood twenty feet apart, tapered down to a width of only nine inches at the floor and made the interior an enchanted landscape unto itself, independent of the city.[9]

[9]Wright, *An Autobiography*, p. 472; in the *Architectural Forum* 94 (January 1951), n.p.; in the *Architectural Forum* 68 (January 1938), p. 88. Also see Jonathan Lipman, *Frank Lloyd Wright and the Johnson Wax Buildings* (New York, 1986).

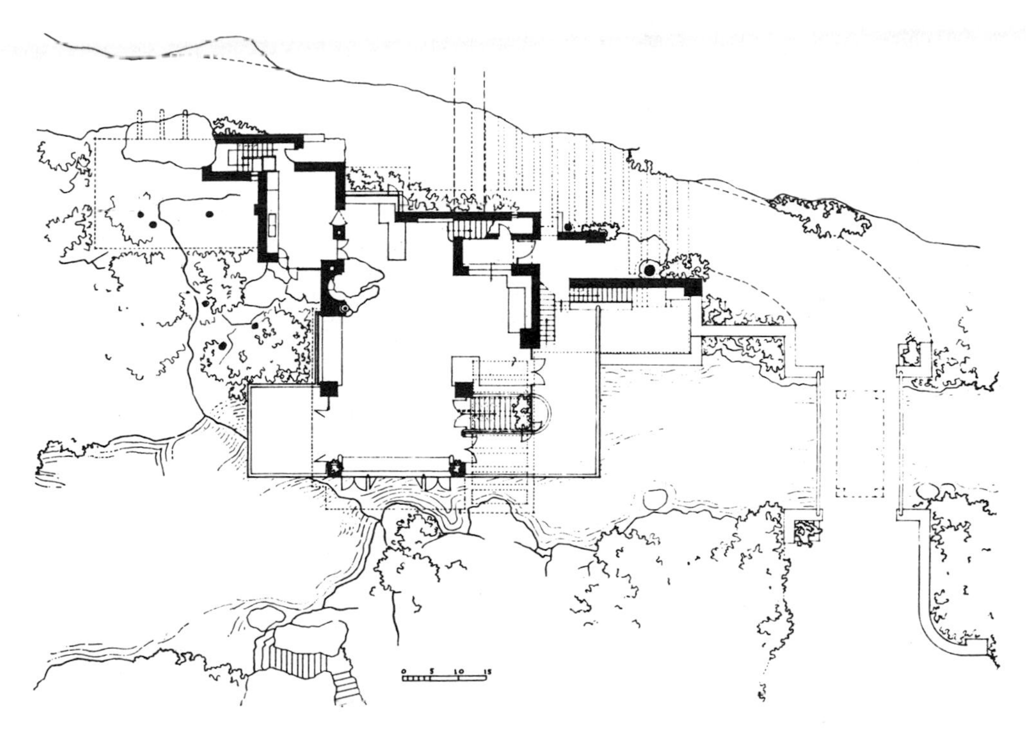

Opposite: **116.** The diversified wall. Fallingwater, view toward entrance. *Above:* **117.** The diversified wall. Fallingwater, first-floor plan.

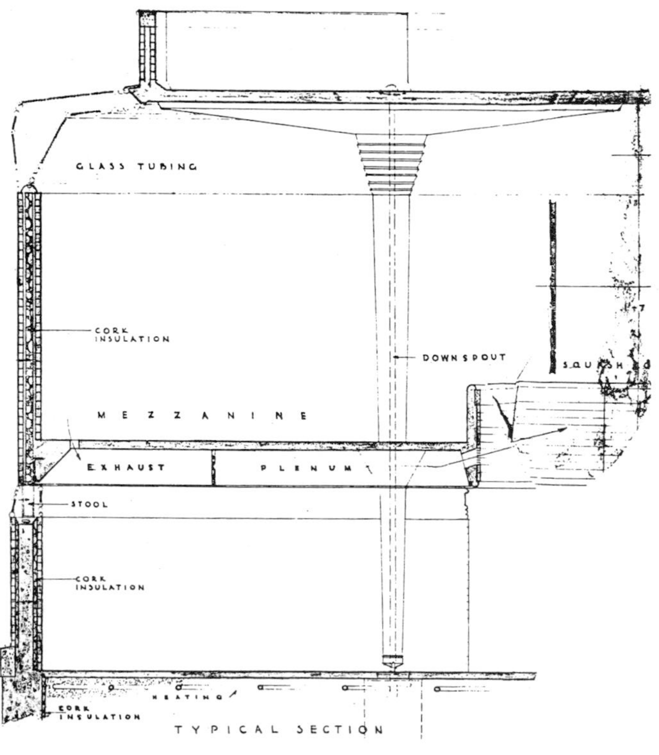

Above: **118.** Glass-filled rifts. Johnson Wax Building in Racine, Wisconsin, 1936–39. *Left:* **119.** Walls as mere screens. Johnson Wax Building, typical section. *Opposite:* **120.** Interior landscape. Johnson Wax Building, great workroom.

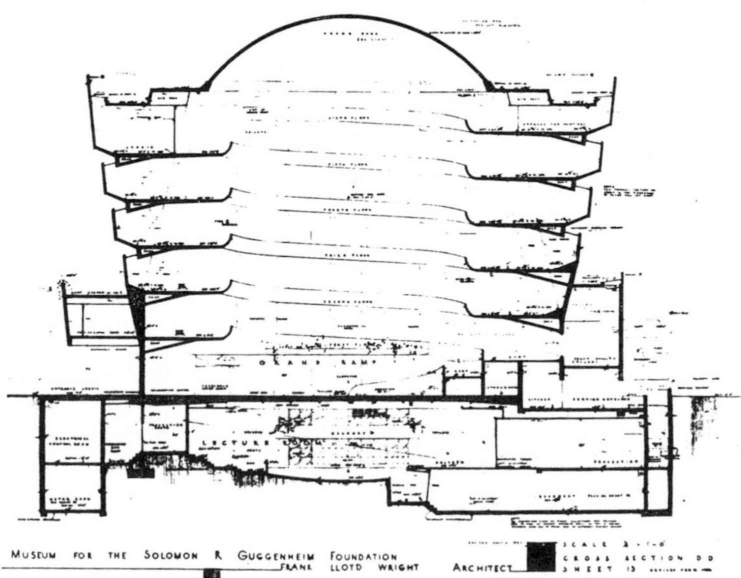

Above: **121.** The spiral ramp. Guggenheim Museum in New York, 1943–59. *Left:* **122.** The continuous internal cantilever. Guggenheim Museum, preliminary section. *Opposite:* **123.** Cantilevers and rifts. Guggenheim Museum, interior.

Wright pursued the same "unlimited overhead" in the Johnson Wax Building as he had in Unity Temple, thirty years earlier. Likewise, the most significant building of his old age, the Guggenheim Museum in New York, could be recognized as the metamorphosis of a spiral ramp he had designed in 1924–25 for the Gordon Strong Automobile Objective and Planetarium [121]. He simply put the ramp indoors and turned it upside down, making it a continuous internal cantilever. The spiral, wider at the top than at the bottom, began its downward path from the elevator destination [122]. Once again, a continuous glass-filled rift expressed the idea. From the top down; at last Wright made fully explicit his earliest principle. Now the light-screen appeared as the dome, conceived as an eye on the sky and originally designed in a graceful pattern of circles immeasurably more appealing than what was built. Wright again achieved the unlimited overhead, and because the spiral ramp continuously departed from the horizontal, he conquered even the tyranny of regularly superimposed floors [123].[10]

---

[10] *Frank Lloyd Wright Preliminary Studies 1889–1916*, ed. Yukio Futagawa (Tokyo, 1985), p. 52.

AN IDIOCENTRIC WORLD

Most of what was paradoxical in the architecture of Frank Lloyd Wright came from the same tension in relation to nature that inspired his work to begin with. For it was not an easy project to emulate the high level of aesthetic organization in nature or to seek through geometric abstraction a reconstitution, or analogue, of the landscape. Such lofty ambitions also helped explain Wright's eccentric manner of self-presentation, from which in fact almost every premise of his architecture could be inferred [124]. A typical pose could signify all at once the robust outdoorsman, artist-architect, noble individualist, lone frontiersman, apostle of the cantilever (as expressed by the pine branch under which he loved to stand) and poet of democratic vistas.

The premises constituted a body of romantic and mutually sustaining values that Wright intended his architecture to champion: a sense of the ground, of shelter, of structural principle and finally of visual form in the service of spaciousness and freedom. First the ground, he said, because the landscape represented man's original home. What was any building as architecture, he asked, without an intimate relation to the ground? "The nature of the site, of the soil and of climate comes first," he wrote. A building in league with the ground would always be valid.[1]

Shelter was both a necessity and an opportunity. Expressed romantically, a sense of shelter could exalt the outdoors. "I think he must love the south in some way," wrote the Viennese architect Richard Neutra, who had studied Wright's work only through pictures:

> In Wright's buildings I have the inmost feeling that man in the beginning lived in a warm climate, and that the greatest, most harmonious and most beautiful people didn't live around fireplaces and didn't die in bedrooms.

The fireplaces in truth were focal points of comfort, warmth and light—indoor analogues of the sun, in buildings conceived in the spirit of pavilion and terrace, what Wright described as "broad shelter in the open":

> . . . already a sense of cleanliness directly related to living in sunlight is at work in us and working not only to emancipate us from the cavern but wak-

[1]Wright, *Architecture and Modern Life*, p. 120; in the *Architectural Forum* 68 (January 1938), pp. 1, 3. Also see Wright, *The Disappearing City* (New York, 1932), p. 40; *An Organic Architecture*, p. 9; *A Testament*, p. 219.

Opposite: **124.** The frontiersman. Wright at Taliesin.

Left: **125.** The open-air spirit. Midway Gardens in Chicago, 1913–14. *Below:* **126.** The open-air spirit. Como Orchard Summer Colony cottage, about 1909.

> ing in us a desire for the substance of a new and more appropriate simplicity as the countenance of building construction . . ..

Hence his imagination, as in the Midway Gardens, favored the architecture of leisure; notably high among his early successes stood the Lake Mendota Boathouse, the River Forest Golf Club and the projects for the Wolf Lake Amusement Park, Yahara River Boathouse and Como Orchard Cottages [125, 126].[2]

Wright could now embody in building the best thought of his time. Viollet-le-Duc and Ruskin, who wrote about architecture with such passion, he had greatly admired; but he also favored Emerson, Thoreau and Whitman, who celebrated nature and the American landscape in opposition to the miseries of the modern industrial city. A taste for the beautiful, Thoreau said, could be cultivated best in the open air:

> Man was not made so large limbed and robust but that he must seek to narrow his world, and wall in a space such as fitted him. He was at first bare and out of doors . . .. Consider first how slight a shelter is absolutely necessary.

[2]McCoy, *Vienna to Los Angeles*, p. 126; *Frank Lloyd Wright on Architecture*, p. 179; "Two Lectures on Architecture," p. 90.

Whitman championed the "fields of freedom" and also wrote that democracy "most of all affiliates with the open air, is sunny and hardy and sane only with Nature." And then there were Wright's colleagues: Louis Sullivan held democracy to be the open-air spirit of responsible freedom, and Jens Jensen founded a school named The Clearing to disseminate, he said, "the message of the great out of doors in its various moods as a fundamental principle to all arts and clear thinking."[3]

From the very first, Wright recognized American life as essentially secular. The "other world" had been ceded to the devout and the superstitious. If buildings were to honor nature and growth, or the inherent and evidently democratic expansiveness of the organic, then they should find their place in the sunlit landscape:

> By means of glass something of the freedom of our arboreal ancestors living in their trees becomes a likely precedent for freedom in twentieth century life . . . it is by way of glass that the sunlit space as a reality becomes the most useful servant of a higher order of the human spirit . . . free living in air and sunlight.

Hence still another paradox. An architecture that drew such strength from revealing the nature of materials and from manifesting the contest between load and support at the same time gloried in the benedictions of light, the only fact of the visible world to appear immaterial and thus free from gravity.[4]

Wright's relation to nature grew complex and ambivalent. At first he looked to nature with modesty, as in 1896:

> Say to yourself: my condition is artificial. So I cannot copy Nature and I will not slavishly imitate her, but I have a mind to control the shaping of artificial things and to learn from Nature her simple truths of form, function, and grace of line.
>
> Nature is a good teacher. I am a child of hers, and apart from her precepts cannot flourish. I cannot work as well as she, perhaps, but at least can shape my work to sympathize with what seems beautiful to me in hers.

And in 1908 he wrote that buildings should form "the background or framework for the human life within their walls and a foil for the nature efflorescence without." When, however, he added that any building should be "complementary to its nature-environment," he implied that nature was not quite complete. Some of his buildings on

---

[3]Thoreau, *Walden*, pp. 125–26; Whitman, "Democratic Vistas" [1871], in *The Portable Walt Whitman*, p. 327; Whitman, *Autobiographia*, as quoted in the *Craftsman* 3 (November 1902), p. 120; Sullivan, *Kindergarten Chats*, p. 15; Leonard K. Eaton, *Landscape Artist in America* (Chicago, 1964), p. 216.

[4]Wright, *An Autobiography*, p. 339.

He also speaks of "this interior concept of lived-in space playing with light"; see *Frank Lloyd Wright on Architecture*, p. 190. Light is not free from gravity; the theoretical conclusion by Einstein that a beam of light bends in a gravitational field was verified by astrophysical observations of light from stars deflecting slightly around the sun.

dismal city sites already had proved they could take the place of nature. He wrote later of his own home in Wisconsin as "a great clarifier and developer of the beauty of landscape," and boasted that the Herbert F. Johnson house, north of Racine, as if by "magic" brought charm and life to an uninteresting place. Although in 1929 he wrote Lewis Mumford that the aim of art was nothing less than "the creation of man as a perfect follower of nature," he had said many years earlier that true aesthetic simplicity required "evidence of mind." Nature exercised "no freedom of choice." Its innumerable exemplars of beauty in structure and form constituted only an "underworld of architecture"; even the greatest natural landscape formations were "not architecture at all." To build was thus "to create a memorial to the power of human imagination." Imagination would inevitably compare its products to those of instinct. "One repays a teacher badly," Nietzsche had said, "if one always remains nothing but a pupil." In his finest efforts Wright competed face to face with nature.[5]

Man did not choose where, or when, to be born or whether to be born at all. Once born, he nonetheless possessed an awe-inspiring faculty. Through his godlike powers of imagination, Wright said, man was capable of getting himself born again and again into the guise of an idealized self. "A creative being is a God," he asserted even in 1927, at the nadir of his career. "There will never be too many Gods." As a creator, he said, man performed as "nature's higher nature," which made architecture "a higher type and expression of nature by way of human nature." Wright had finally arrived at Kant's insight: Genius itself, as an innate productive ability, belonged to nature, and it was through genius that nature gave the rule to art.[6]

Now the heliocentric world shone on the idiocentric, the idea that man stood as the plumb line and always at the center of his own world. Wright especially admired those who affirmed his own sense of the idiocentric, or what he called the "illustrious *sovereignty of the individual*." Nietzsche said the "ripest fruit is the *sovereign individual*, like only to himself"; Wright also found the idiocentric championed by Thoreau, Emerson and Whitman. Emerson warned that society everywhere conspired "against the manhood of every one of its members." He defined character as "nature in the highest form," and wrote of the world as "this shadow of the soul, or *other me*." Thoreau could fancy himself the owner of various farms: "Wherever I sat, there I might live, and the landscape radiated from me accordingly." Whitman called democracy the purport and aim of all the past, and said its end was to demonstrate that man could become a law, and series of laws, unto himself:

---

[5]Wright, "Architect, Architecture, and the Client," p. 31; "In the Cause of Architecture," p. 162; *Modern Architecture*, pp. 65–66; in the *Architectural Forum* 68 (January 1938), p. 3; *An Autobiography*, p. 478; *Letters to Architects*, p. 143; "The Art of Craft of the Machine," p. 64; *Architecture and Modern Life*, p. 44; *His Living Voice*, p. 168; *An Autobiography*, p. 309; *Modern Architecture*, endpapers; Nietzsche, *Thus Spoke Zarathustra*, p. 78.

Wright's attention to nature helped shape his work in many ways: see my study, *Frank Lloyd Wright: Architecture and Nature* (Dover, New York, 1986).

[6]Wright, *Modern Architecture*, p. 43; "In the Cause of Architecture—Fabrication and Imagination," the *Architectural Record* 62 (October 1927), p. 318; *Frank Lloyd Wright on Architecture*, p. 194; *Architecture and Modern Life*, p. 42; Immanuel Kant, *Critique of Judgment* [1790], tr. W. S. Pluhar (Indianapolis, 1987), p. 174.

Wright's son John Lloyd Wright, also an architect, once remarked that "In the large sense no man ever creates anything"; see the exhibition catalogue for "The Midway Gardens 1914–1929" (Chicago, 1961), p. 8.

> What do you suppose creation is?
> What do you suppose will satisfy the soul, except to walk free and own no superior?
> What do you suppose I would intimate to you in a hundred ways, but that man or woman is as good as God?[7]

Wright learned from nature to see all form as a matter of structure and consequence of principle. In the cantilever principle he found a thoroughly natural and radical basis of structure fully able to express the expansive spirit of the sovereign individual. The essence of all true culture, he said, was the development of self-expression. Nature itself had placed a premium on individuality:

> Individuality is the most precious thing in life, after all—isn't it? An honest democracy must believe that it is . . ..
>
> In any expression of the human spirit it is principle manifest as character that alone endures. Individuality is the true property of character.

The prairies had disappeared. So had the Indians and the entire frontier, all in the years when Wright was young; and it was in Chicago, in 1893, that the young historian Frederick Jackson Turner spoke so eloquently of frontier life. The frontier, he said, had nurtured the intellectual traits typical of the expansive American character: individualism, restless energy, the buoyancy and exuberance associated with freedom. It was easy, even plausible, for Wright to see himself as both a pioneer and an indigenous American. So he liked to think of his studio-homes in Wisconsin and Arizona as experimental outposts that kept alive the frontier spirit of freedom; and, to everyone else, he recommended the same way of life. "Again the pioneer takes his place on the frontier," he said of Broadacre City, his project for an idealized exurban America.[8]

Jens Jensen spoke of the "vast open spaces where the horizon seems to touch the earth and where freedom speaks louder than anywhere else in the world." Wright paid homage to the prairies in a new architecture inspired by the horizontal. His instincts called for a virile architecture—"the male nature," he said, "is the projecting nature"—to propel the inner life of a building far into the landscape [127]. Thus he found the cantilever the "most romantic, most free, of all principles of construction." To manifest the inherent tension

[7]Wright, *A Testament*, p. 60; Nietzsche, *Genealogy of Morals* [1887], in *Basic Writings of Nietzsche*, tr. Walter Kaufmann (New York, 1968), p. 495; "Self-Reliance," in *Emerson's Essays* (New York, 1926), p. 35; "Character," *ibid.*, p. 336; "The American Scholar," in *The Portable Emerson*, ed. Mark Van Doren (New York, 1946), p. 32; Thoreau, *Walden*, p. 165; Whitman, *Leaves of Grass* (New York, 1891–92), p. 305; *The Portable Walt Whitman*, p. 330; *Leaves of Grass*, p. 304.

Wright occasionally uses the term *egocentric*, but to avoid the pejorative sense of that word I have chosen a neologism, *idiocentric*.

[8]Wright, "Chicago Culture," p. 155; *An Autobiography*, pp. 560, 233; F. J. Turner, "The Significance of the Frontier in American History," *American Historical Association, Annual Report* (Washington, 1893), passim; Wright, *The Living City* (New York, 1958), p. 114.

Wright's longstanding identification with the Indian reached such a pitch in the 1920s that Erich Mendelsohn found him at Taliesin wearing bark shoes and carrying a tomahawk.

127. Into the landscape. Taliesin, birdwalk.

between load and support was to create a spirited equilibrium between the need for shelter and the desire for outdoor freedom. Hence, with perfect accuracy, he could speak of making "this manly home a refuge for the expanding spirit of man the individual."[9]

He projected an idealized self to make the world into something very much his own. He meant to "take the American ideal of freedom from the realm of human consciousness to our specific expression of that consciousness we call architecture." All the values in his architecture thus took form for the eye to see. "Let a man build," he said, "and you have him." Frank Lloyd Wright accomplished what Louis Sullivan could only forecast—not a simple or prescriptive style, but a characteristic way of building from principles, an architecture that spoke for the highest ideals in American life.[10]

---

[9]Jensen, *Siftings*, p. 21; Wright, *His Living Voice*, p. 69; *An Autobiography*, pp. 215–16; *The Living City*, p. 233. "The mind of man," Joseph Addison wrote in *The Spectator* No. 412 (June 23, 1712), "naturally hates everything that looks like a restraint upon it, and is apt to fancy itself under a sort of confinement when the sight is pent up in a narrow compass . . .. On the contrary, a spacious horizon is an image of liberty."

[10]Wright, "Two Lectures on Architecture," p. 95; *Modern Architecture*, p. 8. "In nearly all great ages of architecture," Jean Bony observes in *French Gothic Architecture of the 12th and 13th Centuries* (Berkeley, California, 1983), p. 45, "the final aim has been one of spatial magnificence: the creation of some new style of spaciousness." Wright's feeling for spaciousness coincided with his ideas of the American landscape and democracy.

INDEX

(Page numbers in *italics* refer to illustrations only.)